NEW YORK

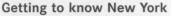

Brooklyn and the Outer Boroughs 156

Lifestyles 172

Accommodation 188

Practical information 192

Surf and go – useful websites 202

Published for WHSmith by Thomas Cook Publishing
PO Box 227
19–21 Coningsby Road
The Thomas Cook Business Park
Peterborough
PE3 8XX
United Kingdom

Tel: 01733 402014
e-mail: books@thomascook.com

Text: © Thomas Cook Publishing 2002
Maps: © Thomas Cook Publishing 2002
Transport map: © TCS

ISBN 1-841572-82-9

Thomas Cook Publishing
Publisher: Donald Greig
Editor: Edith Summerhayes
Picture Researcher: Michelle Warrington
DTP: Steve Collins

Managing Director: Kevin Fitzgerald

WHSmith
Maria Amico
Toby Keir

Original text supplied by: Tony Kelly
This edition up-dated by: Ria Patel

Cover photograph: Getty Images © Joseph Pobereskin, New York City skyline
and highway

WH
S

Destination:
NEW YORK

NEW
YORKER

TONY KELLY

Getting
to know
New York

Discovering New York

Start spreading the news – New York is changing. The city that was a byword for violent crime is now one of the safest places in America. The city whose name was synonymous with sleaze stands accused of turning itself into a family theme park.

What hasn't changed is the sheer restless energy of the world's most extraordinary city, whose very existence is a testament to the power of human ingenuity. Built by Dutch settlers on the tip of a remote island, the city has been reinventing itself ever since with the help of successive waves of immigrants. This is a city where skyscrapers are thrown up only to be demolished 10 years later, a city where this year's *dernier cri* is already next year's antique.

New New York

Half of the world's capital is created here; the city is at the cutting edge of fashion, art and design. At the same time, New York is a city of **neighbourhoods**, once described by Alastair Cooke as 'the biggest collection of villages in the world'. Disney and Warner Brothers may have arrived in New York – but wander into a soul food café in Harlem, or an Italian deli in Brooklyn, and the Mall of America seems a very long way away.

Everyone thinks they know New York. From the movies of Woody Allen to the songs of Billy Joel, from *Guys and Dolls* to *NYPD Blue*, **New York** is embedded in popular culture. We've all seen the Manhattan skyline and climbed the Empire State, even if we've never set foot in the city. We know, or think we do, that the Village is bohemian, the Bronx is dangerous and no one rides the subway after dark. Even New Yorkers think that they know these things. It takes a while to sort out the truth from the urban myths.

Whatever your expectations, New York will surprise you. Yes, the streets are fast and mean, but not *that* fast or *that* mean. And yes, the cops are tough, but then who would be a **New York cop?** Sometimes, with sirens wailing and steam billowing through the sidewalk, the city conforms to all the popular images. At other times, on a quiet stroll beside the Hudson or a misty morning by the Battery, it refuses to be so easily defined. One thing is for certain, New York will never just become Anytown USA. It is too vibrant, too creative, too *different* for that.

New York, New York

New York City consists of five boroughs – Manhattan, Brooklyn, the Bronx, Queens and Staten Island. To most outsiders, New York means the island of Manhattan – also known as New York, New York and immortalised by Frank Sinatra.

A day in the life of New York

As Sinatra sang, New York is the city that never sleeps. If you don't want to sleep either, here is a quick guide to the 24-hour city.

0500 The USA's largest fish market, in the shadow of Brooklyn Bridge, is open all night but the busiest time is as dawn breaks over Manhattan. These days the fish arrives on refrigerated trucks rather than boats.

0800 Farmers from New Jersey and New York State are setting up their stalls at the Union Square Greenmarket, which takes place four times a week.

The working day

0900 Commuters pour out of crowded subway trains and into the Financial District as the world holds its breath for the start of the day's trading on Wall Street. Meanwhile, in Battery Park, the tourists are queuing for the first boat to the Statue of Liberty. Miss this one and you will never make it to her crown.

1200 Secretaries and movie stars spend their lunch hour jogging in Central Park, where you just might catch a glimpse of Madonna in her trainers or Yoko Ono tending the John Lennon memorial garden. Media execs do power lunches at Tavern on the Green – America's busiest restaurant.

1500 Rollerbladers, buskers and students gather in Washington Square, the best spot in the city for people-watching. Once the seedy haunt of pushers and pimps, the square has been cleaned up in recent years and now provides safe family entertainment.

1730 Manhattan's single professionals return to their Upper West Side apartments, stopping off at Zabar's for seared salmon and fresh pasta. Others head for Barnes and Noble, New York's biggest bookstore and pick-up joint, for cappuccino and flirtation among the magazines.

The Staten Island ferry

1830 The romantics take their new date for a ride on the Staten Island Ferry, as the sun sets over the harbour and the skyline lights up for the night. Others stroll across Brooklyn Bridge and along the promenade before dinner with a view at the River Café.

2100 This is the time to take a walk along the inviting Brooklyn promenade that stretches from Brighton 15th St and Bridgewater Ave to West 37th St and the Sea Gate residential colony in Coney Island. The promenade offers a spectacular view of Manhattan.

Nightlife

2200 Straight bars, gay bars, transvestite bars, jazz and swing … if you're looking for nightlife, look no further than Greenwich Village.

Gotham City

It was the author Washington Irving who first named New York 'Gotham City', after a village in England whose inhabitants were said to act like fools in order to discourage visitors.

2300 Another night ends on Broadway and the audiences spill into Times Square, or pop into the Virgin Megastore to pick up a few CDs.

0200 A post-clubbing crowd heads for Florent, in the heart of the newly hip meatpacking district where the porters are already starting work. As the day ends for one set of New Yorkers, for another it is just beginning.

0330 'It is 3.30 in the morning and I am the only one in this subway station and I'm scared' – graffiti found on the subway in 1970.

Yesterday and tomorrow

The first settlers on Manhattan were probably Algonquin Indians, who named the island Manna-hatta, 'island of hills'. But from the moment that the Florentine merchant Giovanni da Verrazano sailed into New York harbour in 1524, the city was destined to be conquered by Europeans.

It was the Dutch who got there first, establishing the trading post of New Amsterdam in 1625 and striking the best property bargain in history when they bought Manhattan from the Indians for 60 guilders' worth of trinkets – only to throw it all away when they swapped Manhattan for Surinam under a treaty of 1667. By then the city was already in British hands, having been surrendered without a fight three years earlier. The British wasted no time in naming the city New York, after the Duke of York, brother of Charles II.

A century of British rule came to an end in 1783, when New York was the final British stronghold to surrender after the War of Independence. **George Washington** marched triumphantly into the city, which briefly became the capital of the new United States. The first **stock exchange** was founded on Wall Street and Manhattan's grid system was laid out. The 19th century saw the start of mass **immigration** to New York, beginning with Irish and German families fleeing famine and continuing with Italians, Jews, Russians and Chinese. By the end of the 19th century the Lower East Side had become the world's most crowded slum – but the building of Brooklyn Bridge and the arrival of the Statue of Liberty gave New Yorkers something to smile about.

New York is born

New York City was created in 1898 by the union of Manhattan with Brooklyn, the Bronx, Queens and Staten Island – a decision still known in Brooklyn as 'the Great Mistake'. The appearance of the Flatiron Building in 1902 signalled the start of the great era of skyscrapers, as Manhattan built ever upwards to absorb a rising population.

The Wall Street crash of 1929 briefly brought Depression, followed by the Golden Age of the 1950s; but a new crisis occurred in the 1970s when the city hovered on the brink of bankruptcy. The 1980s were the age of **yuppie excess**, epitomised by the lavish lifestyle of Donald Trump and the cocaine culture of Jay McInerney's novels. The election of Rudy Giuliani as mayor in 1993 was followed by a rapid drop in crime, a clampdown on drugs and prostitution and the revitalisation of run-down areas like Times Square, Harlem and the Hudson River piers.

The New York Stock Exchange led the 1929 Wall Street Crash.

Clean-up campaign

As New York has entered the new millennium, the clean-up campaign continues. In his attempt to create a new, **tourist-friendly New York**, Giuliani even had the city's legendary hot-dog carts in his sights. Gentrification continues to spread, to the East Village and the Lower East Side and to trendy new acronyms like NoLiTa (North of Little Italy). Harlem is so fashionable that some residents fear for the area's identity. As rents in SoHo and Chelsea climb into the stratosphere, **the art scene**, always a barometer of change, is moving across the water to Brooklyn.

The Big Apple

Contrary to popular belief, New York's nickname was not invented by jazz musicians but by the horse-racing writer John Fitzgerald, who christened the city The Big Apple in his first column for the New York Morning Telegraph *in 1924.*

And what of Manhattan's skyscrapers, and the '**city in the sky**' that people have been predicting for so long? Engineers are at work on a revolutionary elevator that will be able to travel horizontally and diagonally between buildings. The New Yorkers of the future may never have to step out onto the streets. The city could just go on getting higher and higher.

People and places

*'The man who dies rich dies disgraced', said the steel magnate **Andrew Carnegie (1835–1919)**, and he certainly did his best to ensure that it would not happen to him. During his lifetime, he gave away $350 million to found 281 public libraries and a further $2 million for the building of Carnegie Hall. His relatively modest mansion on Fifth Avenue is now the Cooper-Hewitt National Design Museum.*

Serious money

Carnegie was just one of many industrialists who saw their wealth as an opportunity for philanthropy. His great rival Henry Clay Frick (1849–1919), who once said that he would 'meet Carnegie in hell', left his home and his collection of Old Masters to the public. And where would New York be without the **Rockefeller family**? The founder of the oil dynasty, John D Rockefeller (1839–1937), gave away more than $500 million. His son, John D Rockefeller Jr (1876–1960), gave New York the Cloisters, the Rockefeller Center, the Riverside Church and the land for the United Nations. One of his sons, Nelson, became Governor of New York State and Vice-President of the USA; another, John D Rockefeller III, founded the Lincoln Center.

Contrast this with the attitudes of **Donald Trump**, the property speculator said by many to symbolise the greed of the 1980s. At his peak he was worth $1.3 billion. His chief contributions to the city were the Trump Tower shopping mall and the Wollman skating rink in Central Park. Twice divorced and heavily in debt, critics would say he has got what he deserved.

Power politics

Rudolph Giuliani, son of an Italian immigrant from Brooklyn, became New York's first Republican mayor for 28 years when he was elected in 1993. His 'quality of life' campaign is largely credited with the dramatic fall in crime rates and the clean-up of notorious areas like Times Square. Everyone has strong views about Giuliani – some see him as a saviour, others as a busybody who wants to take the fun out of New York. However, his popularity ratings shot up after the terrorist attack on the World Trade Center, because of his on-hands approach and sensitivity in dealing with the devastating consequences. His second term expired in 2001 and he is thought to be planning a shot at the presidency. The new mayor is Michael Bloomberg.

Books, music and films

Woody Allen, born Allen Stewart Konigsberg in Brooklyn in 1935, epitomises the stereotype of the neurotic, sex-obsessed, Jewish New Yorker. This image largely derives from his semi-autobiographical films, such as *Annie Hall* and *Manhattan*, of which he is writer, director and star. He lives in a penthouse overlooking Central Park and plays the clarinet each Monday night at the Café Carlyle.

The director **Martin Scorsese** has portrayed the dark side of Manhattan in films such as *Mean Streets* and *Taxi Driver*, while Spike Lee's tragi-comic films, among them *Do The Right Thing*, deal with challenging issues such as racial tensions in Brooklyn.

Norman Mailer (born 1923) is the greatest living New York author, first coming to prominence in 1948 with *The Naked and the Dead*. In the 1950s he helped found the radical newspaper *Village Voice*, and in 1969 he ran for mayor. Married six times and a fierce critic of feminism, he lives in a brownstone mansion in Brooklyn Heights.

The singer and pianist **Billy Joel** lives on Central Park South, and Manhattan is a recurring theme in his songs, from *52nd Street* to *Uptown Girl* and *New York State Of Mind*. But perhaps the biggest musical influence to have emerged from New York in recent years is hip-hop, born in the ghettos of Harlem and the Bronx in the 1970s.

Annual events and festivals

Because of the many different types of people in New York, its music, food and cultural events are diverse and vibrant. Throughout the year New York City sees a variety of festivals and events. In spring, there are blossoms and tulips in all the parks and the spectacular Macy's Easter Flower Show. 5th Avenue goes completely green for St Patrick's Day and attracts thousands of people. Come summer, and there are many open-air concerts and theatre. Dates of these events may vary but the Visitors' Center on 7th Avenue will provide an updated list of events when you visit them.

January

- (*mid Jan*) National Boat Show at the Jacob Javits Convention Center
- (*late Jan*) Chinese New Year
- Winter Antiques Show, the City's most prestigious antiques fair

February

- Black History Month (African–American events throughout the City)
- (*early Feb*) Empire State Building Run Up – runners race up to the 102nd floor

March

17 St. Patrick's Day Parade
25 Greek Independence Day Parade
- (*Mar–mid April*) New York City Opera spring season
- (*week before Easter*) Easter flower show at Macy's

April

- (*late Apr–May*) Cherry Blossom Festival
- (*Apr–May*) Baseball season starts for the Yankees and the Mets
- (*Apr–June*) New York City Ballet Spring Season

May

5 Cinco de Mayo Festival on 5th Avenue
- (*mid May*) 9th Avenue Street Festival, a feast of ethnic foods, music and dance.
- (*third Sun*) Martin Luther King Jr Day Parade

June

- (*first Sun*) Puerto Rican Day Parade
- (*late June*) Lesbian and Gay Pride Day Parade
- (*late June–early July*) JVC Jazz Festival

July

4 Macy's Firework Display on the East River to celebrate Independence Day.
- (*mid July–mid Sept*) Chinatown Cultural Festival
- (*late July–early Aug*) NY Philharmonic Parks Concerts

August

- (*mid Aug*) Harlem Week
- (*mid Aug–early Sept*) Lincoln Center out-door Festival
- (*late Aug–early Sept*) US Open Tennis Championships

September

- (*all Sept*) American Football season begins for Giant and Jets
- (*Labor Day weekend*) West Indian Carnival in Brooklyn
- (*second Mon*) One World Festival

October

31 Halloween Parade in Greenwich Village
- (*last Sun of Oct/first Sun of Nov*) New York City Marathon
- (*Oct–Jan*) Big Apple Circus at the Lincoln Center

November

- (*fourth Thurs*) Macy's Thanksgiving Day Parade
- (*Nov–Jan*) Christmas star show at the Hayden Planetarium

December

- (*mid-Dec*) Messiah sing-in at the Lincoln Center
- (*New Years Eve*) Fireworks display in Central Park, festivities at Times Square, 5-mile run in Central Park, Poetry reading in St. Mark's Church

Arrival and getting around

Airports

International flights arrive at **John F Kennedy** (JFK) Airport in Queens or **Newark** in New Jersey. From JFK, the quickest way into Manhattan is to take a taxi, for a set rate plus bridge and tunnel tolls and a tip. Uniformed dispatchers will guide you towards the taxi stand and issue a leaflet outlining costs and regulations. Always take a licensed New York City taxi, painted yellow; if you take one of the 'gypsy cabs' which tout for custom at the airport, you may be taken for a ride in more ways than one.

A free shuttle bus connects JFK to Howard Beach subway station, where you can pick up the A train for Brooklyn and Manhattan. You get all the way into the city for the price of a subway token, but it will take at least $1^1/_2$ hours and could be awkward with heavy luggage. An in-between option is to take one of the private bus services which run directly into Manhattan. **Carey Buses** have regular departures for Grand Central Terminal and other points in midtown; **Gray Line** will also stop at downtown and midtown hotels. This is more expensive than the subway, but cheaper than a taxi and has the advantage of door-to-door service.

Taxis from Newark (which is outside the confines of New York City) may be any colour, but again it is important to wait in the official line and not to accept a lift from anyone who approaches you in the terminal. Alternatively, there are regular **bus services** to Grand Central, Penn Station and the Gray Line shuttle to downtown and midtown hotels.

Both JFK and Newark are huge international airports, with several terminals spread out over a wide area. When leaving New York, if travelling by public transport it is important to leave enough time for your bus to reach the right terminal. To be on the safe side, allow an extra 30 minutes.

Most domestic flights arrive at **La Guardia** in Queens, the closest airport to Manhattan. Taxis and Gray Line shuttle services are available, but the cheapest way into town is on the M60 bus, which crosses the Triborough Bridge into Manhattan and connects with the various subway lines along 125th Street.

JFK
Tel: 718–244–4444.
La Guardia
Tel: 718–533–3400.
Newark
Tel: 201–961–2000.

The subway

Let's get one thing straight from the start. The subway is the quickest, most efficient and cheapest way of getting around New York. It runs 24 hours a day and, yes, it is safe to travel after dark as long as you follow a few simple rules. After midnight, stay by the token booth with the other passengers until your train arrives, then head for the conductor's car in the middle of the train. Don't worry about the 'drunk' slumped across the opposite seat, it's probably

an **undercover police officer**. If you find yourself alone in a carriage and feeling uncomfortable, simply get out and move at the next stop.

Everyone travels by subway, from businessmen to bums. The biggest hassles are crowded rush-hour trains and local trains which suddenly turn into an express and whizz through the next six stations just when you wanted to get off. In Manhattan, the most important thing to remember is whether you are going **uptown** (Bronx-bound) or **downtown** (Brooklyn-bound). Almost all lines travel up and downtown; to switch between east and west, take the 42nd Street shuttle between Grand Central and Times Square.

A flat fare applies on all subway rides. You can still buy single-ride subway tokens but these are fast becoming collectors' items as everyone switches to the new magnetic **Metrocards**, which are also valid on buses. These can be loaded in advance with payment for up to 60 rides, though if you're in New York for a week and plan to use the subway regularly, a seven-day

unlimited Metrocard is better value, or a $4 one day unlimited metro card.

Buses

These are fine if you're not in a hurry, but incredibly frustrating if you are. One advantage of buses over the subway is that there are more crosstown routes – though as Manhattan is only two miles wide, it may be quicker to walk. **Bus maps** are available from subway stations and the Visitors' Bureau in Columbus Square. Two of the most scenic and enjoyable rides are the M4 from the Empire State Building to Washington Heights and the Cloisters, and the M5 from Greenwich Village to Riverside Drive.

Taxis and limousines

Everyone has their own story about New York's taxi drivers. They don't understand English; they haven't heard of Canal Street; they never have change for a 20-dollar bill. It is true that many cab drivers are recent immigrants

(*tel: 212–302–8294*). Gypsy cabs, which are unlicensed, are best avoided. Lost and found 212–302–8294.

If several people are travelling together, it may be worth hiring a **limousine**. For upwards of six people, a couple of hours in a stretch limo can be considerably cheaper (and a lot more fun) than a bus tour. Ask your hotel concierge to book you a limousine, or try **Passion Limo** (*tel: 718–739–3366*) or **Zip Connection** (*tel: 212–545–0404*). Bell Radio Taxi 212–691–9191.

whose knowledge of Manhattan's street map is rudimentary, but with a little bit of help most will get you to your destination quickly and for a reasonable charge. **Licensed cabs** are metered, with the fare varying according to distance travelled and time spent in traffic. Drivers will expect a tip of at least ten per cent – though you are in no way obliged to tip – and if you are going outside Manhattan you are also responsible for paying any bridge and tunnel tolls that you incur.

You can hail a taxi on the street when the central numbered portion of the roof light is lit; if the entire light is lit, the driver is off duty. At busy times it is often quicker to walk into a big hotel and out again into the taxi queue.

Cab drivers are obliged to give you a smoke-free, noise-free ride if that is what you want; they are also obliged to take you anywhere within the five boroughs, even if you do want to go to Coney Island at midnight. Licensed taxis, which are yellow, have a medallion number on the roof and a driver's licence number on the dashboard; write these down and if you have any complaints, call the **NYC Taxi and Limousine Commission**

Driving

Don't even think about it. As Mignon McLaughlin once said: 'A car is useless in New York, essential everywhere else. The same with good manners.' In 1998 a columnist on the *New York Times* tried driving the route of the New York Marathon a day after the runners had finished and it took him a good half-hour longer than the race winner. You will never get anywhere and your nerves will be permanently scarred. Enough said?

Walking

Unlike other American cities, Manhattan seems designed for walking. From 14th Street to Central Park, the streets are laid out in a grid system with 'streets' running from east to west and 'avenues' from north to south. The only major exception is Broadway, an old Indian trail which refuses to conform.

Tip

Go to NYC's official visitor **Information Center**, 810 Seventh Ave, at 53rd St (*tel: 212–484–1222*) for free brochures, maps, discount coupons, updates and tickets.

Addresses are given as both an avenue and a street so it is easy to work out exactly how many blocks you are from your destination and in which direction. Allow one–two minutes per block if heading up or downtown, five minutes crosstown between avenues. Above Union Square, 4th Avenue becomes Park Avenue, which runs parallel to Lexington and Madison between 3rd and 5th. Otherwise, everything is pretty straightforward – as long as you remember that 6th Avenue is *always* 6th Avenue and *never* Avenue of the Americas.

Roosevelt Island

For views of Midtown Manhattan, take the cable car to Roosevelt Island, travelling high above the East River. The cars depart every 15 minutes from the corner of 2nd Avenue and East 60th Street.

New York's drivers are not known for their patience with pedestrians, so keep your wits about you when crossing the streets. It is technically illegal to cross at a 'Don't Walk' light. But as everybody says: 'If it says walk, you walk; if it says don't walk, you run.'

Boat trips

The **Staten Island ferry** (*page 159*) is an essential New York experience – and it's free. For a longer ride, take a three hour cruise around Manhattan with **Circle Line**

(*tel: 212–563–3200*), which departs from Pier 83 on West 42nd Street.

Guided tours

One way of seeing all the sights is on an open-top bus tour. **New York Apple Tours** (*tel: 212–944–9200*) has a full range of tours, from a four-hour city tour to a Harlem Gospel Express. Other tours are operated by **Gray Line** (*tel: 212–397–2600*) and **New York Double Decker** (*tel: 212–967–6008*).

Look in Friday's *Weekend* section of the *New York Times* for details of guided neighbourhood walks. Some of the best are those run by the **Municipal Arts Society** (*tel: 212–935–3960*). **Heritage Trails** (*tel: 212–269–1500*) run walking tours of the Financial District, while **Radical Walking Tours** (*tel: 718–492–0069*) offer an alternative view of the city.

A growing number of tours specialise in New York's ethnic neighbourhoods. Operators include **Big Onion Walking Tours** (*tel: 212–439–1090*), **Harlem Spirituals** (*tel: 212–391–0900*), **Braggin' About Brooklyn** (*tel: 718–771–0307*), **Brooklyn Attitude** (*tel: 718–398–0939*) and **Hassidic Tours** (*tel: 718–953–5244*).

Don't miss

1 Statue of Liberty and Ellis Island

A close-up look at America's most powerful symbol and a moving museum recalling the experiences of New York's immigrants – plus magnificent views of the Manhattan skyline from the water. **Pages 30–31, 36–37**
Quick visit: 1 hour; leisurely tour: 1 day.

2 Greenwich Village

Known to New Yorkers simply as 'the Village', this neighbourhood of ivy-covered cottages has long attracted writers, artists and bohemians – as well as a large gay community. **Pages 62–63**
Quick visit: 2 hours; leisurely tour: 1 day.

3 Empire State Building

Since the World Trade Center was destroyed by a terrorist attack on 11 September 2001 the Empire State Building is once again the tallest building in New York. This landmark Art Deco skyscraper offers bird's-eye views of Manhattan.
Pages 78–79
Quick visit: 30 mins; leisurely tour: 1 hour 30 mins.

4 Fifth Avenue

All the famous names of fashion crammed into ten blocks of consumer heaven in the most expensive stretch of commercial real estate in the world. Come here to gawp at the supermodels stepping out of limos into Cartier, Gucci and Tiffany's. **Pages 91, 106**
Quick visit: 1 hour; in depth tour: 5 hours.

5 Museum of Modern Art

All the major painters of the 20th century are represented in this stunning modern art collection. The sculpture garden makes a peaceful retreat and a setting for open-air concerts in summer. **Pages 94–95**
Quick visit: 3 hours; leisurely tour: 6 hours.

6 Times Square

Critics complain that it has lost its edge, but this neon-lit crossroads at the heart of the Broadway theatre district still sets the pulse racing – even if the peep shows have given way to themed souvenir stores. **Pages 100–101**
Quick visit: 1 hour; leisurely tour: 4 hours.

7 Metropolitan Museum of Art

You need at least two visits to get the most out of this museum, with its world-famous collections of Egyptian art, European Old Masters, musical instruments, armour and American period rooms. **Pages 118–119**
Quick visit: 3 hours; in depth tour: 1 day.

8 Central Park

This green space at the heart of Manhattan is where the city comes to walk, jog, ride bikes and row boats, swim in summer, ice-skate in winter and fall in love at any time of year. **Pages 134–135**
Quick visit: 1 hour; leisurely tour: 1 day.

9 Harlem

The spiritual home of black America is undergoing a second Renaissance as affluent black professionals return to their roots and tourists discover the attractions of gospel music and soul food. **Pages 146–147**
Quick visit: 4 hours; leisurely tour: 1 day.

10 Brooklyn Bridge

The world's first steel suspension bridge is not just a remarkable feat of engineering, but a structure of lasting beauty and the classic way to approach Manhattan on foot. **Page 162**
Quick visit: 15 mins; leisurely tour: 1 hour.

The Empire State Building, the Museum of Modern Art, the American Museum of Natural History, Intrepid Sea Air Space Museum and Guggenheim Museum are included in the City Pass. Visit all five and you will save around 50 per cent on admission costs as well as avoiding ticket queues. The City Pass is available at all five sights and can also be bought online at www.citypass.net/ny.

Lower Manh
and the Har
Islands

Lower Manhattan is where it all began. This is where Dutch traders established New Amsterdam, where the British invented New York, where George Washington became the first president of the United States. There is no better place to begin an exploration of the city. Lower Manhattan is the essence of New York, a place where high finance mixes with low life and skyscrapers seem to grow out of the sea.

attan
our

LOWER MANHATTAN AND THE HARBOUR ISLANDS

BEST OF

Lower Manhattan and the Harbour Islands

Getting there: Virtually all of the main subway lines pass through Lower Manhattan; useful stations include Wall St, City Hall, Bowling Green and South Ferry. Alternatively, take the subway to Brooklyn and walk back over Brooklyn Bridge, which ends on the Manhattan side near City Hall. The area is a lot quieter at weekends, when the Financial District shuts up shop – but the downside is that several of the attractions are closed.

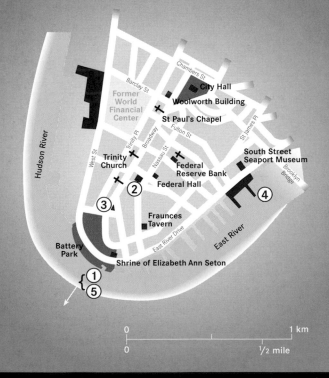

① Ellis Island

A visit to this fascinating museum is essential to understand the experiences of the 12 million immigrants who passed through its doors – and who have done so much to shape 21st-century American life.
Pages 30–31

② New York Stock Exchange

The decisions made on Wall Street reverberate around the world and you can watch the chaos as it unfolds from a viewing gallery above the trading floor. Just try not to think about your pension. **Page 33**

③ National Museum of the American Indian

This challenging museum, in the grand setting of the former Customs House, adopts a refreshingly different perspective – looking at the customs and lifestyles of America's Indians through their own eyes. **Page 34**

④ South Street Seaport

The heart of the 19th-century seaport, once the greatest in the world, has been rejuvenated as a vibrant area of shops, restaurants and museums, just the place to come on a summer afternoon. It is also home to the city's largest fish market. **Page 35**

⑤ Statue of Liberty

An inspiring symbol of freedom or a monumental piece of kitsch? It all depends on your point of view. But there is no doubt that this is one of New York's must-see sights – as the queues for the boat trip testify.
Pages 36–37

Battery Park

Subway: 1, 9 to South Ferry; 4, 5 to Bowling Green.

This 23-acre park, built on landfill at the southern tip of Manhattan, is named after the battery of cannon which once protected the city from assault. The Dutch built their first fortress here and called it Fort Amsterdam; the current fort, Castle Clinton, dates from 1811. When it was first built, the castle was 200 ft offshore and was connected to Manhattan by a causeway. Built to

defend the city from a British invasion fleet that never arrived, the fortress fell into disuse until it was given new life as the Castle Garden entertainment centre, where opera and theatre were performed and P T Barnum put on lavish shows. From 1855 to 1889 it was New York's immigration centre, processing some eight million arrivals. Later, Castle Clinton became the New York Aquarium – until it was closed down in 1941 and threatened with demolition by the building of the Brooklyn–Battery Tunnel.

Today Castle Clinton still stands, preserved as a national monument and used as a National Parks visitor centre. A booth sells tickets for the ferry to Ellis Island. During the day, Battery Park is awash with souvenir stalls and sightseers queueing for the boats. At night, when the tourists have gone home, or at dawn, as the mist rises over Liberty in the harbour, it can be one of the most atmospheric places in New York.

Battery Park City

Subway: 1, 9, N, R to Rector St or Cortlandt St.

Like its namesake, Battery Park City was created out of landfill – in this case
the rubble left over from the building of the World Trade Center and dumped
into the Hudson River. Conceived in the 1980s as an ambitious business and
residential complex which would put the soul back into Lower Manhattan, it
is often described as the Rockefeller Center for the 21st century. At the heart
of the 'city' is the World Financial Center, where four uneven glass towers are
set around the Winter Garden, a dazzling public space of upscale restaurants
and shops given an exotic touch by the introduction of 16 imported palm
trees. From here, a mile-long esplanade beside the Hudson offers clear views
of the Statue of Liberty and the commuter ferries heading for New Jersey.
This is postmodern architecture on a human scale.

The **Museum of Jewish Heritage**, opened in 1997 in a hexagonal
structure based on the Star of David, is dedicated to the history of the
Holocaust. *Museum of Jewish Heritage, 18 First Place, Battery Park City.
Tel: 212–509–6130; www.mjhnyc.org. Open: Sun–Wed and Fri 0900–1700,
Thur 0900–2000. Admission: **.*

City Hall

Subway: 4, 5, 6, N, R to Brooklyn Bridge–City Hall.

Crossing Brooklyn Bridge into Manhattan, you arrive at City
Hall Park, at the centre of which is City Hall, completed in 1812.
During the week, it is usually possible to visit the Governor's
Room, where receptions for visiting heads of state are held.
Outside City Hall is a statue of Nathan Hale, hanged by the
British as a spy in 1776. His last words were: 'My only regret is
that I have but one life to offer in the service of my country.' Also
in 1776, City Hall Park was the setting for the first public reading in New
York of the Declaration of Independence – an act of defiance to the British
ordered by George Washington.

" *Sometimes, from beyond the skyscrapers, the cry of a tugboat finds you
in your insomnia, and you remember that this desert of iron and cement
is an island.* **"**
Albert Camus (1913–60)

Ellis Island

If your ancestors arrived in America by boat, you will find a visit to Ellis Island an intensely moving experience. Between 1892 and 1924, more than 12 million immigrants passed through its doors in the largest migration in human history.

The first was a 16-year-old girl from County Cork in Ireland, coming to America to join her parents; later arrivals included Bob Hope, Irving Berlin and Rudolph Valentino. Most were admitted to the land of their dreams; an unfortunate two per cent were sent 'home' on the next ship.

Golda Meir, a Russian Jewish migrant who passed through Ellis Island in 1906 and later became prime minister of Israel, said that 'going to America was like going to the moon'. Many of the refugees were fleeing poverty and persecution and saw in America the opportunity of a new

life. After gruelling journeys on crowded ships, their fates were often decided in a six-second medical examination, with chalk marks scratched on their clothing to indicate any grounds for suspicion.

In theory, until 1921, the United States operated an open-door policy; in practice there were numerous restrictions. Legislation was introduced to exclude first convicts and prostitutes, then coolies and eventually idiots, paupers, epileptics, polygamists, beggars, anarchists and illiterates. As **refugees** from southern and eastern Europe outnumbered the earlier Irish and German **immigrants**, there were racist attempts to exclude 'inferior, undesirable and unintelligent' types. Politicians spoke of the dregs of Europe coming to New York. Prospective immigrants were caught in a trap – they had to prove that they would not 'become a public charge' but if they said that they had a job to go to they would be barred as 'contract labourers'.

The full story of the millions who passed through Ellis Island is told with the help of artefacts, photographs and the oral histories of 1700 immigrants. Stand in the **Great Hall**, the vast hangar where fates were decided, staring through the windows at Manhattan across the water, and try to imagine how it felt to be waiting in line. See the **'Stairs of Separation'**, where so many families were divided, and the **'Kissing Post'**, where successful applicants were reunited with their loved ones. A matron recorded their reactions: 'The Italian kisses his little children but scarcely speaks to his wife … the Jew kisses his wife and children as if he had all the kisses in the world, and intended to use them all up quick.'

Ellis Island was abandoned in 1954 and stood in ruins for many years before being carefully restored and opened as an **immigration museum** in 1990. More than 100 million Americans can trace their ancestry to this place. The American Immigrant Wall of Honor, in the gardens, contains the names of some half a million of them, a physical reminder of the sheer scale of the immigrant contribution to American society.

> " *When the immigrants came, as they sailed through the Narrows, past the Statue of Liberty, it was as if New York Harbor was America's box office and the curtain just going up on a new life.* "
>
> **Reggie Nadelson, whose grandparents arrived at Ellis Island in 1901, writing in the** *Independent*, **1995**

Getting there: By boat from Battery Park. Boats depart every 30 minutes from 0930–1530 in summer, less often in winter (for details call 212–269–5755). Open: 0930–1700 daily. www.ellisisland.org. Admission included in ferry ticket.

Financial District

The origins of Wall Street lie in the low wooden wall erected by the Dutch in 1653 at the northern boundary of New Amsterdam. Nowadays, 'Wall Street' refers to the entire Financial District, an area roughly bordered by Broadway, Beaver Street, Pearl Street and Maiden Lane. This is the nerve centre of the world's financial markets; for five days a week it is a hive of frenetic activity, then an eerie calm descends at weekends.

Federal Hall

26 Wall St. Tel: 212–825–6870. Open: Mon–Fri 0900–1700. Regular guided tours. Admission free.

This Greek Revival building, designed as the US Customs House in 1842, stands on the site of the original City Hall where George Washington gave his inaugural presidential address in 1789. The building was renamed Federal Hall and served as the US Capitol for a year. It is now a museum devoted to the American constitution; among the exhibits are the suit worn by Washington for his address and the Bible on which he took the oath of office.

Federal Reserve Bank

33 Liberty St. Tel: 212–720–6130. Free hour-long guided tours are available if booked a week in advance. Open: Mon–Fri 0830–1700.

" *Mammon, n. The god of the world's leading religion. His chief temple is in the holy city of New York.* **"**

Ambrose Bierce, The Devil's Dictionary, 1911

This neo-Italian palazzo with a façade of Ohio sandstone holds a third of the world's gold reserves in its underground vaults. If you are fascinated by money, you will love it here. Upstairs, dirty money (the average dollar bill lasts about 18 months) is shredded at the rate of $40 million a day; five floors down, the gold ingots are protected behind 90-ton doors. Workers in magnesium shoes used to physically transfer the blocks of gold between vaults whenever international transactions were made. Not surprisingly, security here is extremely tight.

New York Stock Exchange

20 Broad St. Open: Mon–Fri 0900–1630 (tickets available 212–656–5168). Admission free.

What began in 1792 as 24 brokers trading stocks beneath a buttonwood tree has grown into a state-of-the-art facility

where 200 million shares change hands electronically each day. Half of all the world's capital is generated in this one building. Just occasionally things go horribly wrong. The Wall Street crash of 1929, when the Dow Jones index dropped 11 per cent in a day, plunged New York (and the world) into Depression; 'Black Monday' in 1987 signalled the end of the 'greedy Eighties'.

Get here early to beat the queues; the start of the day's trading is the best time to watch. A small museum explains the history of the Stock Exchange and the changing technology of trading. As you stand in the viewing gallery, watching the traders scurrying around like excited schoolboys, try not to think that it might be your investments they are playing with.

Trinity Church

Broadway at Wall St. Tel: 212–602–0872. Open: Mon–Fri 0700–1800, Sat 0800–1600, Sun 0700–1600.

When the present Gothic Revival church was consecrated in 1846, it was the tallest building in Manhattan; now it is dwarfed by the cathedrals of finance around it. This is the third church on this site – the original one was completed in 1698 under charter from William III of England. The graveyard contains the remains of numerous early New Yorkers, including Alexander Hamilton, the first Treasury Secretary, and William Bradford, founder of New York's first newspaper – as well as the oldest carved tombstone in the city, dated 1681 and dedicated to a five-year-old boy.

Fraunces Tavern

54 Pearl St. Subway: 1,9 to South Ferry; 2, 3 to Wall St; 4, 5 to Bowling Green; N, R to Whitehall St. Tel: 212–425–1778. Open: Tue–Fri 1000–1645, Sat–Sun 1200–1600. Admission: *.

This museum of early American history is housed in a reconstructed 18th-century tavern, built by a former mayor's son on what was then the Manhattan shore. The inn was acquired by the patriot Samuel Fraunces; as the Queen's Head, it became a notable meeting place for opponents of British rule. Following victory in the War of Independence, George Washington bade an emotional farewell to his troops in the Long Room, now faithfully restored in period design. The pub downstairs still serves its original function and is a popular lunchtime haunt of Wall Street executives.

National Museum of the American Indian

1 Bowling Green. Subway: 4, 5 to Bowling Green; 1, 9 to South Ferry. Tel: 212–668–6624. Open: Fri–Wed 1000–1700, Thur 1000–2000. Admission free.

As you approach this fine Beaux Arts building, designed by Cass Gilbert in 1907 as the US Customs House, the first thing you notice is the set of four female sculptures representing the continents (America, Europe, Africa and Asia) according to the prejudices of the day. Asia is meditative; Africa is asleep; Europe is surrounded by former glories; America looks forward with an Indian at her feet. Nothing could be less in tune with the message of the museum inside.

The museum, based on the collection of George Gustav Heye, an investment banker who became fascinated with native American culture, deliberately sets out to challenge and provoke. Art is presented as art, not as natural history or anthropology; native curators have been invited to choose and interpret the exhibits. Sacred and funerary objects are displayed only with the approval of the ethnic group in question, and many have been returned to the descendants of their original owners. Attitudes have moved on since Heye was allowed to 'collect' Indian artefacts on his travels. The exhibits include everything from prehistoric stone carvings to contemporary silkscreen prints, but far more interesting is the way they are brought alive by the voices of native Americans themselves.

South Street Seaport

Subway: 2, 3, 4, 5, J, M, Z to Fulton St. Tel: 212–748–8600.
www.southstreetseaport.com. Museum open: daily 1000–1700, 1000–1800
in summer. Admission: **.

To some this is the most vibrant place in Manhattan; to others an example of crass commercialism. This great East River seaport was in danger of disappearing altogether until a group of citizens in the 1960s decided to give it a new lease of life. As with waterfront developments elsewhere, the result is an eclectic mix of museums, restaurants and shops set in and around the old piers, warehouses and saloons. The handsome 19th-century warehouses along Schermerhorn Row are now fish restaurants and trendy pubs; Pier 17, at the heart of the complex, is little more than a shopping mall with great views of the Brooklyn Bridge. But the presence of the Fulton Fish Market, in business since 1822, prevents the area from becoming a mere theme park, and the museum, with its historic ships and displays of boatbuilding, provides a link with the city's maritime history. This is a great place to spend some time in summer, when street entertainers, lunchtime concerts and harbour cruises all add to the festive waterfront atmosphere.

> **"** *There is something in the New York air that makes sleep useless.* **"**
>
> **Simone de Beauvoir,**
> ***America Day By Day**, 1953*

Statue of Liberty

Woody Allen quipped that she was the first woman to allow him inside her; the anarchist Emma Goldman wept when she saw 'the symbol of hope'. Liberty Enlightening the World, *to give her her full title, continues to inspire cynicism and emotion in equal measure.*

Conceived by French Republicans as a monument to their missing freedoms, the statue became a gift to the American people in commemoration of shared democratic ideals. The sculptor, Auguste Bartholdi, had initially envisaged a statue at the entrance to the Suez Canal, but soon realised the symbolic value of New York harbour as a gateway to the free world.

The statue, thought to be based on Bartholdi's mother, was more than ten years in the making; the frame was designed by the engineer Gustave Eiffel. The figure is heavily loaded with symbolism, from the torch and crown to the broken shackles at her feet and the tablet containing the Declaration of Independence in her left hand. Completed in 1886 at a time of mass immigration, Liberty soon became a defining symbol of the new opportunities offered by America. Over the years she has become the universally recognised icon of 'the land of the free'.

A selection of letters from immigrants, on display inside the statue, describes the emotions that many felt as they sailed into the harbour for the first time and were greeted by Liberty's shining torch. The theme of immigration was taken up by Emma Lazarus, in the poem written to raise funds for the statue's base and now engraved on the pedestal:

Give me your tired, your poor,
Your huddled masses yearning to breathe free,
The wretched refuse to your teeming shore.
Send these, the homeless, tempest-tost to me,
I lift my lamp beside the golden door.

" *Viewed from underneath, a hugely pregnant housewife in a nightgown and brandishing a candlestick, Liberty's expression was blank, her features vaguely sneering, with a sullen twist to her thick lips – a dead ringer for early Elvis.* **"**

Nik Cohn, *The Heart of the World*, 1992

It is difficult not to be impressed by the sheer size of the statue, the greatest metallic figure ever built. Close up, it is just so much bigger than it looks across the water. The torch is 305 ft above the sea; the statue alone is 151 ft high; her finger is 8 ft long and her nose a full 4.5 ft. If you really want to, you can climb up to her crown, though the queues are such that you will need to catch the first boat of the day and it will probably take you two hours. Most people settle for an elevator ride to the tenth-floor observation deck, with its panoramic views of New York harbour. Make time, too, to visit the museum exploring the statue's history and iconography – and to look at the original torch, on display in the lobby. As part of the restoration work for the statue's centenary in 1986, a new gilded copper torch was installed according to Bartholdi's original design.

This trip should be combined with a visit to Ellis Island (*pages 30–31*). Go early and allow a full day.

Getting there: By boat from Battery Park (details as Ellis Island). Admission included in ferry ticket.

St. Paul's Chapel

Broadway and Fulton St. Subway: 2, 3, 4, 5, J, M, Z to Fulton St; A, C to Broadway–Nassau St. Tel: 212–602–0874. Open: daily 0900–1500.

This tranquil oasis in the heart of downtown Manhattan is one of New York's few remaining examples of colonial architecture. Built in 1766 on a field outside the city, it was designed as a 'chapel-of-ease' for the parish of Trinity Church (*page 33*). The architect, Thomas MacBean, modelled the chapel on the church of St. Martin-in-the-Fields in London. The feathers of the Prince of Wales adorn the pulpit and the original cut-glass chandeliers from Waterford hang in the nave. George Washington worshipped here on the day of his inauguration and his pew has been preserved beneath an oil

painting of the presidential seal commissioned for the inaugural service. The peaceful churchyard, previously in the shadow of the World Trade Center, features monuments to Revolutionary heroes and to a popular Shakespearian actor, George Frederick Cooke.

Woolworth Building

233 Broadway. Subway: 2, 3 to Park Place; N, R to City Hall. Open: Office Hours.

> **"** *The most truly civilized of the earth's cities . . . where mankind has, for good or for bad, advanced furthest on its erratic course through history.* **"**
>
> **Jan Morris, *Manhattan*, 1979**

When it was completed in 1913, this 60-storey Gothic skyscraper was the tallest in New York and the second tallest structure in the world, surpassed only by the Eiffel Tower in Paris. It was officially opened by President Woodrow Wilson, who flicked a switch in Washington illuminating 80,000 light bulbs on the building's exterior – an effect that was seen

100 miles out at sea. The building, designed by Cass Gilbert, was conceived as a 'Cathedral of Commerce' by Frank Winfield Woolworth, who made his fortune by founding the celebrated five-and-dime stores. You can walk into the lobby during office hours to admire the gold mosaic ceilings and the playful gargoyles of Gilbert holding a model of the building and Woolworth counting out his coins. Woolworth paid $13.5 million for the building in cash and this was no doubt Gilbert's way of paying him back.

World Trade Center – Ground Zero

The tragedy of the 11th of September 2001, a date now synonymous with the Twin Towers when two fuel-laden hijacked planes crashed into and destroyed the World Trade Center, continues to have a massive effect on the people of New York, America and the world as a whole. Such great feelings of loss are very much apparent in the area that has now been renamed Ground Zero.

The World Trade Center was built as a result of a massive urban renewal project sponsored by the Port authority of New York. Begun in 1966 and completed in 1970, the 16-acre site became the centre of international trade and commerce. The Towers had become the two tallest buildings in New York (having 110 storeys each) and a strong symbol of America's power and wealth.

There are discussions on placing a memorial statue in the centre of Ground Zero for people to visit and pay their respects. It will stand as tribute to the thousands who lost their lives and those who lost family and friends.

To read more about the attack and the Trade Center itself, visit www.worldtradecenternewyork.com

The Manhattan skyline

'The Americans have practically added a new dimension to space', wrote William Archer in 1899. 'When they find themselves a little crowded, they simply tilt a street on end and call it a skyscraper.'

If only he could see Manhattan today. Since the completion of the **Flatiron Building** in 1902, the race has been on to build bigger and better. **The Woolworth, Chrysler** and **Empire State buildings** and the **World Trade Center** (New York's tallest building until it was destroyed by terrorists on 11 September 2001) were all at one stage the tallest buildings on earth.

The classic image of the New York skyline is the view of **Lower Manhattan**, seen across the water from **Brooklyn** or the **Staten Island ferry**. At first all you see is the big picture, a thicket of steel and glass – but look carefully and you soon pick out hidden details. There is a spot on the **Brooklyn Heights Promenade** where it is just possible to peer down Wall Street and make out **Trinity Church**, once Manhattan's tallest building.

There are good views of **Midtown** across the East River, from the derelict piers of Greenpoint and the cable car to **Roosevelt Island**. The Midtown skyline is dominated by the Art Deco towers of the Empire State and Chrysler buildings, glistening in the sun by day and spectacularly lit up at night. The sheer glass wall of the UN Secretariat rises above the waterfront, and the slanted roof of the **Citicorp Center** – Manhattan's most striking example of postmodern architecture – draws your gaze north.

" *A hundred times have I thought New York is a catastrophe, and fifty times – it is a beautiful catastrophe.* **"**
Le Corbusier (1887–1965)

To see Manhattan from every angle, take a **Circle Line cruise** (*tel: 212–563–3200*). These start from a pier on the Hudson River (*Pier 83, W 42nd St*) and continue right around the island, up the Harlem River and under the **George Washington Bridge**. All that is missing is the view from above – for which the only option, and the ultimate New York thrill, is a helicopter ride over the skyscrapers. *Tel: 212–355–0801.*

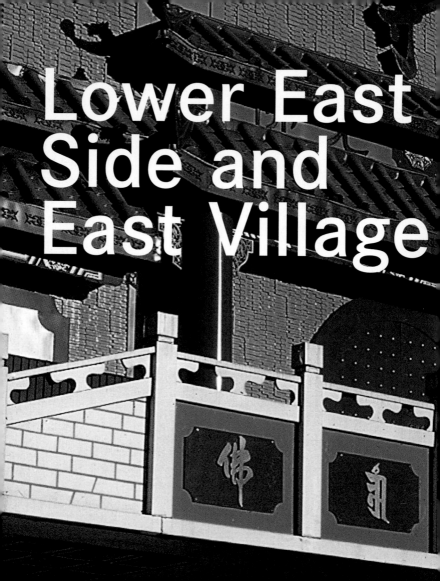

Lower East Side and Side and East Village

This small neighbourhood is the most densely populated on earth, with a character like nowhere else in New York.

LOWER EAST SIDE AND EAST VILLAGE

BEST OF

Lower East Side and East Village

Getting there: **Subway:** *J, M, N, R, Z, 6 to Canal St for Chinatown and Little Italy; B, D, Q to Grand St, J, M, Z to Essex St or F to Delancey St for Lower East Side; L to 1st Ave or 6 to Astor Place for East Village. Avoid Saturdays when the Orchard St shops are closed.*

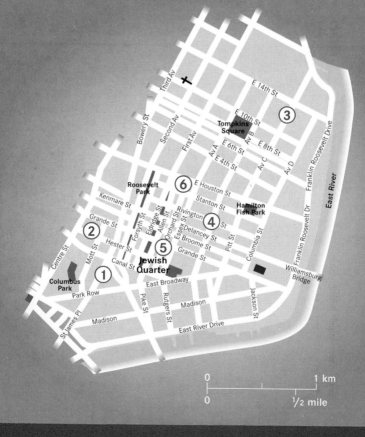

① Chinatown

The largest Chinese community in the Western world is spreading over an ever-increasing area, but the heart of the Chinese district on Mott Street remains a fascinating enclave of Oriental restaurants, herbalists and grocery stores. **Pages 48–49**

② Little Italy

From Fiorello La Guardia to Rudolph Giuliani, Italians have played an important role in New York's affairs, and this area on Mulberry Street is where many of their ancestors made their homes. Come here to eat some of the best pasta in New York. **Page 48**

③ East Village

The notorious Alphabet City has lost its rough edge and New Yorkers now flock to the East Village for its cool clubs, funky shops, ethnic restaurants and alternative lifestyles. **Pages 50–51**

④ Orchard Street

This shopping street at the centre of the old Jewish quarter was the birthplace of New York's clothing industry, where goods made in the local sweatshops were sold from pushcarts in the street. Today the Sunday market captures some of the same flavour. **Page 52**

47

⑤ Lower East Side Tenement Museum

A captivating glimpse into the realities of immigrant life, seen through a visit to one of the area's former tenement buildings and the stories of the people who lived there. **Page 53**

⑥ Katz's Deli

This landmark Jewish deli has become a New York institution, with pictures of presidents and movie stars on the walls. Everyone should come here once to try their famous salami. **Page 55**

Chinatown and Little Italy

'Chinatown is a period over which the alphabet of our city has to step' wrote the journalist Djuna Barnes in 1913. She had gone where few women of her time would have dared to tread, to research an area of the city that was synonymous with gang warfare and danger. Expecting to find 'a crooked street lit with blood-red lanterns … girls who grew old in a year and men who laughed at death' she seemed almost disappointed to have survived the episode unscathed. 'There is no Chinatown' she concluded.

Chinatown is the most complete of Manhattan's ethnic enclaves; more even than Harlem, it has refused to succumb to the outside world. Irish, Italian and Jewish immigrants moved out of the Lower East Side as soon as they could afford to, but the Chinese have stayed together. In fact Chinatown is steadily encroaching on its neighbours: it spills into SoHo and the Jewish district and has virtually taken over Little Italy. Chinese characters adorn the façade of the *Jewish Daily Forward* building, once a Lower East Side landmark and now a Chinese church.

The first Cantonese merchant moved into Mott Street in 1858; within 20 years the Chinese population reached 20,000, of whom 99 per cent were men. This was the time of the Mafia-style Tong wars, fought out by rival Chinese gangs; the corner of Pell and Doyers Streets, where dead bodies were dumped, became known as 'Bloody Angle'. Today's Chinatown is still centred on Mott, Pell and Bayard Streets but with a population of 100,000 it has had to expand. East Broadway is now known as 'Little Fuzhou' after the many illegal immigrants from the Chinese province of Fujian,

some of them smuggled in by 'snakeheads' for extortionate fees. The presence of these new arrivals – and others from Vietnam and Cambodia – has led to an occasional return of the old tensions.

Take a walk up Mott Street to get a flavour of the area. Glazed ducks hang in restaurant windows, pushcarts offer taro root and scallion pancakes, news-stands sell Chinese newspapers and pharmacists weigh out herbal remedies on old-fashioned scales. The Buddhist temple at 64 Mott Street has a wonderfully kitsch giftshop; near by, in Bayard Street, is the Wall of Democracy, with posters and cuttings on contemporary events in China. If you want to do more than just wander, look into the **Museum of Chinese in the Americas** (*70 Mulberry St; tel: 212–619–4785; open Tue–Sat 1200–1700; admission **) to learn about the history of Chinatown. Many Chinese immigrants, as they always have, work in sweatshops and laundries; after seeing this exhibition those jokes about Chinese laundries may have a slightly hollow ring.

At one time New York was home to more Italians than Rome and the area around Mulberry Street was known as **Little Italy**. It still is, though these days there are far more Italians living in Brooklyn and the Bronx (when Martin Scorsese shot *Mean Streets*, about Mafia wars in Little Italy, he had to film it in the Bronx). All that remains of Little Italy is a string of Italian restaurants on Mulberry Street and a handful of delicatessens selling fresh pasta and ricotta cheese. The graveyard of **Old St. Patrick's Cathedral**, on the edge of Little Italy, contains the tomb of Pierre Toussaint, born a slave in Haiti and now a candidate for sainthood.

> " Can we really know the universe? It's hard enough trying to find your way around Chinatown. "
>
> **Woody Allen**

Getting there: Subway: J, M, N, R, Z, 6 to Canal St.

East Village

The East Village is New York with attitude. Anarchists, beatniks, bohemians and punks have long called it home. Ignored even by the subway, the East Village has always offered a refuge to all those who fitted in nowhere else – including communities of Ukrainians, Indians and Poles.

In the 1980s this was where New Yorkers feared to tread. The Bowery was known as the city's skid row. Tompkins Square Park was the scene of pitched battles between police and squatters. Alphabet City, between Avenues A and D, was controlled by crack cocaine dealers and rumours abounded of people who had wandered in and never came out.

There is still a nervous edge to the East Village, a sense that anything can happen and probably will, but for the most part the tension these days is creative. The area around St. Mark's Place, the East Village's main thoroughfare, has become one of the most hip in town and you are more likely to bump into an organic juice bar than a drug dealer. The streets are lined with cybercafés, vegan bakeries, funky boutiques and off-off-Broadway theatres. Body piercing and green-dyed hair are *de rigueur*. Community gardens and arts centres have sprung up in Alphabet City. Even the East River Park, with its industrial views of Brooklyn, has been reclaimed as a place where Puerto Rican families from the local 'projects' go strolling on Sunday afternoons – though it can still be a little scary after dark. The spray-painted portraits on the walls are, after all, of teenage gun victims.

Take the time to visit a pair of historic churches. **Grace Church**, (*802 Broadway*), is a handsome example of Victorian Gothic architecture. The midget General Tom Thumb was married here, in a wedding staged by the showman P T Barnum. **St. Mark's-in-the-Bowery**, three blocks along 10th Street, is one of the oldest churches in Manhattan, on the site of an early Dutch chapel. The first Dutch governor, Peter Stuyvesant – known as 'peg-leg Pete' on account of his wooden leg – built himself a *bouwerie*

(farm) here and refused to return to Holland even after the Dutch moved out. He is buried in the churchyard with seven generations of his descendants. The Beat poets Jack Kerouac and Allen Ginsberg used to give readings in the church and it remains a focus of the radical New York arts scene.

Across the street, the **Tenth Street Turkish and Russian Baths** (*open daily 0800–2200*) is the last of the traditional steam baths which were once scattered all over the Lower East Side. This has become one of Manhattan's hottest places to meet, and not just because of the steam. You can have a massage or a Dead Sea salt body scrub, then fill up with borscht and stuffed cabbage in the restaurant. **Little Ukraine**, around 2nd Avenue, is home to some 30,000 exiled Ukrainians. **The Ukrainian Museum** (*203 2nd Ave; open Wed–Sat 1300–1700; admission* *) features exhibitions of Ukrainian folk costumes and painted Easter eggs. The focus of the Ukrainian community is **St. George's Ukrainian Catholic Church**, which stands opposite **McSorley's Old Ale House**, one of New York's oldest pubs (*page 55*).

" *I'm a New Yorker. Fear is my life.* "

From *Rent* by Jonathan Larson, the 1996 Broadway musical about a group of artists in Alphabet City

Getting there: Subway: L to 1st Ave; 6 to Astor Pl.

Jewish Quarter

Although it has always been inhabited by a mix of nationalities, and although Chinatown is encroaching on one side and Loisaida on the other, the core of the Lower East Side between Houston and Canal Streets has retained its essentially Jewish character. Shops advertise bar mitzvah sets, yarmulkas and kosher food; every bakery

has a sign in the window stating that it is under the supervision of this or that rabbi. The area is home to several New York Jewish icons, from Katz's Deli and Guss' Pickles to Kossar's hot bialy shop and Schapiro's kosher winery (see page 55). These are the streets that spawned George Gershwin and Irving Berlin, the streets where the Marx Brothers cut their teeth. The neo-Gothic **Eldridge Street Synagogue,** *with its stained glass and intricate woodwork, is the spiritual heart of the area and the first house of worship built by East European Jews in New York.*

Most people come here on Sundays, when **Orchard Street** becomes a crowded open-air market, with jeans and fancy dresses hanging from coat racks in the street. It's actually easier to shop here during the week – though remember that the shops shut on Friday afternoon and all day Saturday for the Jewish sabbath. From Lolita's Bras to Sam's Knitwear, almost every shop on Orchard Street specialises in cheap clothes, many of them manufactured in local sweatshops by Puerto Rican and Chinese immigrants. Discounted (and imitation) designer clothes may not be on display, but the trick is to visit a department store, note down what you want, then go to Orchard Street and ask for it.

Getting there: Subway: B, D, Q to Grand St; J, M, Z to Essex St; F to Delancey St.

Lower East Side Tenement Museum

The 19th-century red brick tenement blocks, with their tangles of fire escapes zigzagging down to the street, are a distinctive feature of the Lower East Side and a visit to this absorbing museum gives you the chance to see one from the inside. At one stage these slums housed 1000 people an acre; Charles Dickens said that they made Calcutta look like Paradise. The Danish immigrant Jacob Riis, who slept rough while carrying out his research, described the appalling conditions of the 1890s in his book How the Other Half Lives.

The tenement at **97 Orchard Street** was built in 1862 and housed 120 people in twenty three-room apartments. There was no lighting, heating, water or sanitation; an elevated train ran overhead and the street outside was a red-light district. Infant mortality in the Lower East Side was 40 per cent. Such stark statistics are brought to life by the guides, who reel off fascinating details about the minutiae of everyday life.

> **"** *Everybody ought to have a Lower East Side in their life.* **"**
> **Irving Berlin (1888–1989)**

The **apartments** have been preserved as they were in 1935. One resident, Natalie Gumpertz, was a German dressmaker; you are shown pictures of her great-great-grandchildren, all-American kids from New Jersey. You learn about the Baldizzi family from Sicily, then hear the voice of their daughter, now an elderly woman, as she describes growing up in the tenement. The **guides** point out that many of today's immigrants, Korean doctors and Russian concert pianists, live in not dissimilar conditions. This fascinating museum is a tribute to New York's immigrants, described as the 'urban pioneers' of modern America.

Getting there: 90 Orchard St. Tel: 212–431–0233. Open: Tue–Sun 1300, 1400, 1500, Sat–Sun 1600. Admission: **.

Restaurants

Chinatown

Bo Ky
80 Bayard St. Tel: 212–406–2292.
No credit cards. *. Come here for big
bowls of Vietnamese noodle soup,
topped with duck, pork or shrimp and
served at rock-bottom prices.

Canton
45 Division St. Tel: 212–226–4441.
No credit cards. ***. This is regularly
rated as the top Chinese restaurant in
New York. Don't worry about the
menu; let the manager decide.

Grand Sichuan
125 Canal St (Bowery).
Tel: 212–625–9212. **
Authentic Szechuan food. Come here
for a banquet of spicy, flavourful food.

20 Mott Street
20 Mott St. Tel: 212–964–0380. **.
There are long queues at weekends
for this excellent *dim sum* restaurant,
where you just point to what you want
as the snack carts roll by.

Little Italy

Il Fornaio
132a Mulberry St. Tel: 212–226–8306.
**. No-frills, old-fashioned Italian
cooking – try the baked clams or the
stuffed artichokes.

La Mela
167 Mulberry St. Tel: 212–431–9493.
**. This rowdy Italian eatery serves
great pasta and is always heaving
with local families. There is no menu,
so you have to trust the waiters.

Lombardi's
*32 Spring St. Tel: 212–941–7994. No
credit cards.* *. The birthplace of New
York pizza in 1905 still turns out some
of the best pizzas in town. The regular
'pie' is cooked in a coal oven and
features mozzarella and pecorino
from Italy.

Mexican Radio
19 Cleveland Place. Tel: 212–343–0140.
**. This intimate bistro with candles
on the tables serves great margaritas
and new Mexican cuisine.

Lower East Side/East Village

Katz's Deli
205 E Houston St. Tel: 212–254–2246.
*. This retro Jewish deli has framed
letters from presidents in the window
and ancient signs hanging from the
ceiling exhorting you to 'send a salami
to your boy in the Army'. You could
have what Bill Clinton had (two hot
dogs, a pastrami sandwich and fries)
or even copy Meg Ryan, who famously
faked an orgasm here in *When Harry
Met Sally*.

Riodizio
417 Lafayette St. Tel: 212–529–1313.
**. This trendy 'Central Village' rotisserie
features pitchers of caipirinhas and an
all-you-can-eat Brazilian menu of flame-
roasted meat, fish and vegetables.

Bars and clubs

Café Wha?
115 Macdougal St (between Bleecker and West 3rd Sts). Tel: 212–254–3706. The Cafe Wha? is quite simply the greatest place in New York to hear live music. Featuring the most exciting array of musicians and singers available anywhere, the Wha? has people dancing in the aisles seven nights a week.

CBGB
315 Bowery at Bleecker St. Tel: 212–982–4052. The birthplace of American punk is as loud and raw as ever. Check the listings in the weekly papers.

Dharma
174 Orchard St. This new arrival on the Orchard Street scene has cool jazz, Latin and world music in a former shoe shop.

Idlewild
145 E Houston St. Hip cocktail lounge themed as a 707, with aircraft seats, pilots for barmen and stewardesses serving drinks.

Jewish food

Two unofficial symbols of New York, the bagel and the pastrami sandwich, were introduced on the Lower East Side by European Jews. For bagels and bialys (a Polish onion roll), try Kossar's (369 Grand St). Yonah Schimmel's (137 E Houston St) sells the original knishes filled with buckwheat, potato or cherry, while at Schapiro's House of Wines (126 Rivington St), you can buy kosher sangria, chablis and sauternes.

Kush
183 Orchard St. The décor is rustic Moroccan and the music an eclectic mix at this cool candlelit bar.

McSorley's Old Ale House
15 E 7th St. This pub, in business since 1854, only began admitting women in 1970 after a long legal battle. Office workers come here at the end of the day for corned beef hash and home-brewed beer.

Nuyorican Poets Café
236 E 3rd St. This East Village hangout is the home of the Poetry Slam, offering poetry, hip-hop and multimedia art for a new Beat generation.

Shopping

Canal Street, between Chinatown and SoHo, is where half of the world's fake Rolexes are sold – they fool nobody, but teenagers seem to love them. **Orchard Street** (*page 52*) is the best place for discount clothes, though check out the designer chic at **Klein's of Monticello** (*105 Orchard St*) and the ladies' bags at **Fine & Klein** (*119 Orchard St*) as well. A free Sunday shopping tour of the Orchard Street area leaves Katz's Deli at 1100 every Sunday from April to December. The East Village, between 7th and 9th Streets from 3rd Avenue to Avenue A, is full of wacky clothes shops – one of the hottest is **TG 170** (*309 E 9th St*).

The gorgeous mosaic

It was David Dinkins, New York's first black mayor, who coined the phrase 'gorgeous mosaic' to describe the city's ethnic mix. This is a city where 'native' New Yorkers – those descended from the first European settlers – are in a minority. Irish and German labourers arrived in the 19th century, followed by Italians and East European Jews; the largest groups of migrants these days are from Asia and Latin America. From Korean greengrocers to Orthodox cathedrals, the streets of New York reflect its personality as a city of immigrants. Traditionally, most immigrants have made for the Lower East Side but there are pockets of foreign culture dotted over the city. Try visiting some of these:

Little India, on 6th Street in the East Village, is one of the best and cheapest places in New York to get a curry.

Little Spain, on 14th Street west of 6th Avenue, was settled by Spanish sailors after the Spanish Civil War and still has a sprinkling of Spanish restaurants and tapas bars.

Hell's Kitchen, between Chelsea and Midtown, was a notorious slum once inhabited by Irish navvies. The area has restyled itself Clinton as it develops a more upmarket image.

Yorkville, in the East 80s beside the East River, was settled by Germans and Hungarians and retains a handful of German beer cellars and pastry shops. South of here is an area known as Little Bohemia.

El Barrio is the Puerto Rican district of East Harlem, centred around the vibrant street market known as La Marqueta.

Washington Heights is home to the largest Dominican community in the United States. In the bodegas on Broadway, everyone speaks Spanish.

Greenpoint in Brooklyn is known as Little Poland and neighbouring **Williamsburg** is home to a large community of Hassidic Jews.

Brighton Beach in Brooklyn has become known as Little Odessa because of its growing population of ex-Soviet Jews.

Astoria in Queens has the largest Greek population outside Athens, numbering around 100,000. The tavernas on Broadway sell Greek coffee and stuffed vine leaves.

" *It's not a melting pot, it's a boiling pot.* "

Thomas E Dewey
Governor of New York
in the 1940s

SoHo and Greenwich Village

Two areas that were once threatened with demolition have been spectacularly revived as two of New York's most happening neighbourhoods. The abandoned lofts of SoHo have been transformed into contemporary art galleries, while Greenwich Village is known for its jazz clubs and thriving gay scene. These are places designed for strolling, for casual shopping and long weekend brunches accompanied by the Sunday papers.

SoHo and Greenwich Village

*Getting there: **Subway:** 1, 9 to Christopher St–Sheridan Sq for Greenwich Village; A, B, C, D, E, F, Q to W 4th St for Washington Sq; various lines to Spring St, Prince St or Broadway-Lafayette for SoHo. The best time to visit is at weekends. Most SoHo galleries are open from Tuesday to Saturday.*

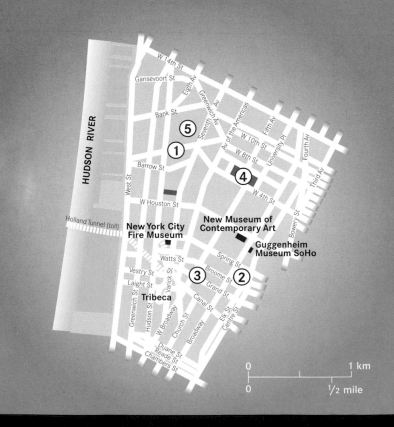

① Christopher Street

Soak up the atmosphere of Greenwich Village in this busy street of florists, cool cafés and raunchy leather shops. The tangle of leafy lanes to the south of Christopher Street is one of the most attractive areas of New York.
Pages 62–63

② SoHo art galleries

SoHo is at the cutting edge of the contemporary art scene and you can visit some of the galleries to get a feel for what's hot. The district also contains Manhattan's alternative 'museum mile', with three modern art museums on one block. **Pages 64–65**

③ Cast-iron architecture

The largest concentration of cast-iron architecture in the world is found in a small area of SoHo around Greene Street. These rare examples of early industrial art provide a historical link to the avant-garde artists of today.
Pages 64–65

④ Washington Square

The unofficial campus of New York University, with an arch modelled on the Arc de Triomphe in Paris, provides the perfect open-air stage for indulging in that old-fashioned pastime of people-watching. **Pages 66–67**

⑤ All that jazz

The jazz clubs of Greenwich Village are the hottest in New York, from big names like the Blue Note and Village Vanguard to smaller places featuring Brazilian blues or zydeco and swing.
Page 68

Greenwich Village

Known to many New Yorkers as the West Village and to most simply as 'the Village', it was Greenwich Village that spawned the Village People (remember YMCA?) and the Village Voice. *The Village came to the world's attention in 1969 when police raided the Stonewall bar, sparking off a violent confrontation and leading to the birth of the worldwide gay rights movement. Today this is one of the most pleasing areas of the city, a place of ivy-covered brownstone houses and quiet back streets, of cafés and florists and a genuinely village-like atmosphere where the only difference is that all the men seem to be holding hands.*

The Stonewall riots are remembered in **Sheridan Square**, where a statue of Civil War hero General Sheridan looks down disapprovingly on more recent statues of a gay and a lesbian couple. **Christopher Street**, leading off from here, is the heart of the gay Village, with leather shops, an erotic bakery and the world's first gay bookshop. If you find a chain store around here it will probably be selling chains.

South of **Christopher Street** is a maze of leafy lanes which resolutely defy the grid system of Manhattan. These streets were once cowpaths in the days when Greenwich was a rural retreat from the city. **Barrow Street**, **Bedford Street**, **St. Luke's Place** and **Gay Street** are all lined with handsome 19th-century houses in Italianate or Federal Revival style. In the 1920s, this area attracted a circle of writers and bohemians including Djuna Barnes, Kahlil Gibran, Emma Goldman, e e cummings and Gertrude Stein. Edna St. Vincent Millay moved into the narrowest house in Manhattan at **75 ¹/₂ Bedford Street**, where she wrote the poem that still acts as a gay anthem in the time of AIDS:

> " *The greater part of New York is as soulless as a department store; but Greenwich Village has recollections like ears filled with muted music and hopes like sightless eyes straining to catch a glimpse of the beatific vision.* "
>
> **Djuna Barnes,**
> **Pearson's Magazine, 1916**

'My candle burns at both ends,
It will not last the night;
But oh my foes and oh my friends –
It gives a lovely light!'

In the 1950s Greenwich Village was condemned as a slum and there were plans to raze it for new housing, until a tireless campaign by local resident Jane Jacobs (author of *The Death and Life of Great American Cities*) led to its being declared a national historic district. Among its landmarks is **Jefferson Market Library**, a Victorian Gothic red brick pile of turrets and gables on 6th Avenue, built as a women's courthouse in 1877. Across the street, **Balducci's** (*page 69*) is one of the finest gourmet food stores in New York.

In the 1990s the Village has gone through something of an identity crisis as its gayness has been diluted by an influx of straight professionals. The outrageous Hallowe'en Parade, which began in 1973 as a purely Village event, now attracts a million New Yorkers and goes out on prime-time TV. At the same time, the Village has drawn both female and transvestite **prostitutes** who have been displaced by the clean-up of **Times Square**. Some residents fear that this is destroying their cherished quality of life; others say that in an atmosphere of tolerance, anything goes.

Getting there: Subway: 1, 9 to Christopher St–Sheridan Sq.

New York City Fire Museum

278 Spring St. Subway: C, E to Spring St; 1, 9 to Houston St.
Tel: 212–691–1303. Open: Tue–Sun 1000–1700. Admission: *.

If the police are New York's Finest, then fire-fighters are New York's Bravest and this museum, in a renovated firehouse on the edge of SoHo, pays tribute to generations of firemen. Among the exhibits is an original horse-drawn fire engine from Brooklyn, a collection of helmets and felt stovepipe hats, and a display of fire insurance marks which New Yorkers used to put up on their houses so that the private fire-fighters would know which buildings were covered by insurance. Too bad if you weren't.

SoHo Cast-Iron Historic District

Subway: C, E to Spring St; N, R to Prince St; B, D, F, Q to Broadway–Lafayette.

The transformation of SoHo (the name means South of Houston Street) is a story that has been repeated in several once run-down areas of New York. In the 1960s, artists – attracted by the low rents and the bright open spaces – began moving into the vacant lofts and industrial warehouses of the area's disused factories. Restaurants and cafés soon followed and before long SoHo was the most fashionable district in town. The result is that few artists can afford to live there any more and everyone complains that SoHo has lost its soul.

The frontiers of the art scene may have shifted to **Chelsea** and Williamsburg, but SoHo remains the nerve centre of the New York art market. A favourite weekend pastime is gallery-hopping. Check out the listings in *Time Out* or Friday's *New York Times*, or pick up a copy of the *Gallery Guide* at any of the major galleries. Most are concentrated in a small area between Broadway and West Broadway, especially along Greene and Wooster Streets. You are welcome to browse, but if you're thinking paintings hanging on walls, think again. Don't be surprised if you are expected to participate in performance art or multimedia installations.

Visit the **Earth Room** (*141 Wooster St*) and you will be confronted by a gallery filled with dirt.

A block of newish museums on Broadway bridges the gap between the formal collections of Museum Mile and the contemporary art scene of SoHo. The **Guggenheim Museum SoHo** (*575 Broadway; open Sun and Wed–Fri 1100–1800, Sat 1100–2000; admission ***) is a branch of its uptown namesake with an emphasis on multimedia art. The **New Museum of Contemporary Art** (*583 Broadway. Tel: 212–219–1222. www.newmuseum.org. Open: Tue–Wed, Fri–Sun 1200–1800. Admission **; free Thur 1800–2000*) showcases some of the more experimental artists, while the **Alternative Museum** (*594 Broadway; open Wed–Sat 1100–1800; Admission **) offers radical social and artistic comment. The **Museum for African Art** (*593 Broadway. Tel: 212–966–1313. Open: Tue–Fri 1030–1730, Sat 1200–2000, Sun 1200–1800; admission **) is the only one of its kind in the city.

65

66 *When it's 9.30 in New York it's 1937 in Los Angeles.* **99**

Groucho Marx (1890–1977)

It was SoHo's artists who campaigned to preserve the late 19th-century cast-iron buildings in which many of their galleries are based. Designed as a means of erecting factories both quickly and cheaply, cast-iron architecture was used to create a whole range of decorative styles. Sweatshops could be adorned with Renaissance façades, or warehouses given a Baroque touch. On Greene Street, 50 cast-iron buildings are found in five cobblestoned blocks; but perhaps the supreme example of cast-iron architecture is the **Haughwout Building**, on the corner of Broadway and Broome Street.

Washington Square

Henry James grew up here and set a novel in one of its 'solid and honorable dwellings'. A century later, Robert Redford and Jane Fonda walked Barefoot in the Park. *In 1995 this was the setting for* Kids, *a cult movie about a group of nihilistic teenagers indulging in drug-crazed orgies and random acts of violence. One way or another, Washington Square has always seemed to sum up the New York zeitgeist.*

Bernard Levin called it 'New York's village green', though there is little that is green about it. What he meant is that this is where New York comes to play. Washington Square is the best open-air show in Manhattan, from the guitarists and street performers to the skateboarders, the dope dealers and the hustlers playing speed chess. Come here on a lazy summer afternoon and it seems as though all of New York is gathered around the fountain. Return in the evening and you might catch a free performance of Shakespeare.

Washington Square, where the West Village begins to merge into the East, started out as marshland and later became the city's burial and execution ground. A 'hanging elm' still stands in the northwest corner and thousands of bodies remain buried beneath the square. It became a public park in 1827 at about the same time as the elegant Greek Revival houses were being built on the north side of the square. Henry James lived in number 18, his grandmother's house, which has since been demolished; another novelist, Edith Wharton, lived at number 1.

The triumphal arch at the foot of Fifth Avenue was designed by Stanford White in 1895, replacing an earlier version built to mark the centenary of George Washington's inauguration. Fred Astaire danced on top of the arch in *The Belle of New York*, and in 1916 one Marcel Duchamp climbed to its summit to declare Greenwich Village 'the free republic of New Bohemia'. By the 1950s the arch was being used as a turnaround point for buses, and Robert Moses, the city planner who changed the face of New York, proposed building a highway through the square. In three decades, this was one of the few battles he did not win. The redoubtable Jane Jacobs, saviour of Greenwich Village, led the campaign against the new road and today Washington Square Park is closed to traffic. It is also a lot safer than it once was. The park is closed at night and can feel slightly threatening after dark, but during daylight hours you will experience a lot more fun than fear.

> *I know not whether it is owing to the tenderness of early associations, but this portion of New York appears to many persons the most delectable. It has a kind of established repose which is not of frequent occurrence in other quarters of the long, shrill city . . .*

Henry James,
Washington Square,
1880

Most of the buildings around the square are used by New York University, the largest private university in the USA. Among them, on the southern side, is **Judson Memorial Baptist Church**, built in Greco–Romanesque style in 1892 in honour of the early American missionary Adoniram Judson, whose Burmese translation of the Bible is set into the cornerstone. The church was intended to bring together the wealthy inhabitants of Washington Square North and the tenement dwellers of the south side; to this day it remains a centre of radical activism on issues from AIDS to unemployment.

Getting there: Subway: A, B, C, D, E, F, Q to W 4th St–Washington Sq.

Restaurants

For an eclectic range of fine dining in intimate surroundings, it's hard to beat Greenwich Village.

Casa
72 Bedford St. Tel: 212–366–9410. **. Come here to experience hearty Brazilian home cooking, such as grilled beef with garlic cloves or the house special, feijoada – a casserole of chorizo, bacon, black beans and salted beef.

Chez Michallet
90 Bedford St. Tel: 212–242–8309. ***. This tiny French bistro has been described as the best place in Manhattan for a first date. The weekend brunch menu features steak au poivre with champagne.

Babbo
110 Waverly Pl (between Macdougal St and 6th Ave). Tel: 212–777–0303. ***. Modern Italian food in a beautiful townhouse setting, Babbo is described as the 'mind-boggling Village teaser'.

Moustache
90 Bedford St. Tel: 212–229–2220. *. The Lebanese salads and pitta-based pizzas are great value at this funky Middle Eastern joint.

One If By Land, Two If By Sea
17 Barrow St. Tel: 212–228–0822. ***. With roaring fires, piano music and creative New American cuisine, this restaurant in a 1726 town house is just the place for a romantic evening.

Pink Teacup
42 Grove St. Tel: 212–807–6755. No credit cards. *. This Village institution serves classic soul food and huge Southern breakfasts, with pecan pancakes, fried chicken, grits, ham and eggs.

Il Mulino
86 W 3rd St. (between Sullivan and Thompson Sts). Tel: 212–673–3783. ***. New York's no. 1 Italian restaurant – come here for huge amounts of heavenly food.

Jazz clubs

Greenwich Village is the centre of the New York jazz scene. Famous names play the **Blue Note** (*131 W 3rd St at 6th Ave*) or the **Village Vanguard** (*178 7th Ave at W 11th St*). **Sweet Basil** (*88 7th Ave at Bleecker St*) features a weekend jazz brunch, while **Smalls** (*183 W 10th St at 7th Ave*) has ten hours of jazz every night. **SOBs** (*204 Varick St at Houston St*) showcases Brazilian, Afro-Cuban and Caribbean bands, and **Louisiana** (*622 Broadway at Houston St*) has zydeco, swing and Cajun cooking – and no cover charge. Check the listings each week in *Time Out* or the *Village Voice*. For a tour of some of the lesser-known jazz clubs, call Jerry Rose on 212–875–7019.

Bars

Chumleys

86 Bedford St., Greenwich Village. The door is still unmarked at this Prohibition era speakeasy, where books by former regulars Ernest Hemingway and Dylan Thomas line the walls. These days it attracts a beer-and-burger college crowd.

Ñ

33 Crosby St, SoHo. Tel: 212–219–8856. New York's coolest tapas bar has a long sherry list and copious pitchers of sangria to accompany the flamenco dancing on Wednesday nights.

Pravda

281 Lafayette St, SoHo. You can play celebrity-spotting at this Russian-themed bar, where fashion models and pop stars linger over caviar and mango-flavoured vodka.

White Horse Tavern

567 Hudson St at 11th St, Greenwich Village. Tel: 212–989–3956. Dylan Thomas drank his final whisky at this far West Village landmark, still going strong and popular with a young crowd.

Shopping

*Manhattan's top flea market, with a wide range of antiques and vintage fashions, takes place each Saturday and Sunday on the corner of Broadway and Grand Street in SoHo. Near here, **Canal Jean Company** (504 Broadway) is a huge warehouse offering brand-name jeans and underwear at discount prices. **Balducci's** (424 6th Ave) and **Dean and Deluca** (560 Broadway) are the top downtown food stores, with ravishing displays of cheeses and fresh produce, while **Myers of Keswick** (634 Hudson St) is a genuine British grocer selling Bovril, Marmite and Ribena to British exiles. For a gift with a difference, how about painting your own pottery at **Our Name Is Mud** (59 Greenwich Ave)?*

The meatpacking district

The latest up-and-coming nightlife area is the meatpacking district around West 14th Street in the 'North Village'. Steak frites with a view of the carcasses may not be quite as romantic as grilled lobster with a view of the sea, but for a mixed crowd of drag queens and post-clubbers coming home from Mother (432 W 14th St), the gleaming chrome French diner at Florent (69 Gansevoort St) is the only place to be at 4.00am.

Gay and lesbian New York

New York's single women are often heard to complain that all the attractive, available men in the city are gay. In a city of eight million people, at least one million are gay and gay men far outnumber lesbians. The gay scene in New York is out in the open – the annual Gay Pride march in June attracts half a million spectators and the Empire State is lit up in lavender for the event. It is sometimes hard to remember that it is only 30 years since police raided the Stonewall bar.

BLEECKER ST

CHRISTOPHER ST

SOHO AND GREENWICH VILLAGE

Although Greenwich Village has long been associated with gay men, the focus of the gay community has shifted in recent years. The locals in the Village have grown tired of being stared at by straight tourists who head there for a glimpse of gay life. The male scene is now centred around Chelsea, especially on 8th Avenue between 14th and 23rd, while lesbians are more at home in the East Village or Park Slope in Brooklyn. Other gay-friendly areas of the city are the Upper West Side and Jackson Heights in Queens.

The most fabulous new additions to the Chelsea Lounge scene include **XL** at *357 16th St* (a total must with happy hour on weekday evenings from 1600 till 2100), and **Heaven**, (no relation to the London Superclub) can be found at *W 19th St/7th Ave*. Slightly more established are **g**, a hunky cabaret lounge at *225 W 19th St* and **Splash** *50 W 17th St* (with bar top showers that gave the venue its name) which are both still big with the locals. For a bit of Latin flavour try another hot spot **La Nueva Escuelita**, a crazy Hispanic drag club open Thur–Sun (*301 W 39th St at 8th Ave*).

For women, go to the Village for **Meow Mix** (*269 E Houston St*), **Crazy Nanny's** (*21 7th Ave*) and for a great Saturday night out go to **Lovergirl** at True (*28 E 23rd St*).

Pick up a copy of *Time Out* New York or *HX* and *HX for Her* as New York Hot spots change frequently, so make sure you get the latest views on what's going on in the city.

For more on New York's gay history, as well as resources on the contemporary gay scene, visit one of the two gay bookshops – **A different Light** (*151 W 19th St*) and the **Oscar Wilde Memorial Bookshop** (*15 Christopher St*).

A governor in drag

New York's reputation for sexual tolerance goes back to 1702, when the British governor Lord Cornbury would flaunt himself on Broadway dressed in women's clothes.

Chelsea and Gramercy

North of 14th Street the grid system takes over as the cosy atmosphere of the Villages gradually gives way to the chaos and corporate culture of Midtown. Between 14th and 34th Streets lie two of Manhattan's most interesting neighbourhoods – arty, sporty Chelsea and quiet, bookish Gramercy Park – as well as two of the city's best-loved skyscrapers.

BEST OF

Chelsea and Gramercy

Getting there: **Subway:** *A, C, E, 1, 2, 3, 9 to anywhere between 14th and 34th Sts for Chelsea; B, D, F, N, Q, R to 34th St for the Empire State and Macy's; L, N, R, 4, 5, 6 to 14th St–Union Sq or 6 to 23rd St for Union Sq and Gramercy Park.*

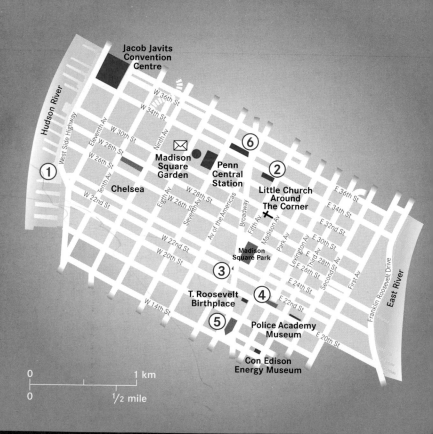

0 — 1 km

0 — ½ mile

① Chelsea Piers

The derelict Hudson River piers have been given a spectacular new lease of life at this sparkling new riverside sports mall. Come here to swim, jog or work out in the gym, then take in a lunchtime concert on the waterfront promenade. **Page 77**

② Empire State Building

This Art Deco skyscraper is a worldwide symbol of New York, towering over its surroundings and offering unbeatable views of the Manhattan skyline day and night. **Pages 78–79**

③ Flatiron Building

This 20-storey skyscraper caused a sensation when it was built in 1902. It may not look much now, but this was the building that ushered in the skyscraper age in New York. **Page 80**

④ Gramercy Park

This peaceful square of 19th-century town houses surrounding a private park has long been one of the most desirable addresses in Manhattan. Numerous authors and artists have lived here. **Pages 80–81**

⑤ Union Square Greenmarket

Flowers, organic vegetables, apple cider and home-baked bread are all on display at the city's largest Greenmarket, where farmers bring their produce to sell direct to the public. **Page 81**

⑥ Macy's

'The world's largest store' takes up an entire block with ten floors of clothing and household goods. Strange to think that it all began in 1857 with Rowland Macy's slogan 'It's smart to be thrifty' and all dealings in cash. **Page 82**

Chelsea

Subway: A, C, E, 1, 2, 3, 9 to anywhere between 14th and 34th Sts.

Chelsea is one of Manhattan's most enjoyable and diverse neighbourhoods. Here you will find markets and trendy restaurants, slaughterhouses and tapas bars, avant-garde art galleries, a riverside walk and an active gay scene. This is New York's gymland, where hunky 'Chelsea Boys' pump iron in window-front displays while simultaneously checking the price of their shares on the Internet. The best way to explore this district is on a gentle stroll from south to north. Begin in the **Chelsea Historic District** on West 20th Street, where the Greek Revival houses on Cushman Row are adorned with pineapples – a traditional symbol of hospitality. Three blocks north, the **Chelsea Hotel** (*222 W 23rd St*) has an air of seedy glamour and decaying Edwardian grandeur that continues to attract writers and artists in search of low life. Brendan Behan, Mark Twain and Arthur Miller all lived here; Dylan Thomas and Vladimir Nabokov were regular visitors. Andy Warhol shot *Chelsea Girls* here in the 1960s, Joni Mitchell wrote *Chelsea Morning* and Sid Vicious of the Sex Pistols stabbed his girlfriend Nancy Spungen to death.

An antiques fair and flea market takes over three blocks of 6th Avenue between 24th and 27th Streets each weekend. Keep going north and 6th Avenue turns into a flower market, at its liveliest in the early morning. Eventually you reach the **Garment District**, the centre of New York's fashion industry, where fabric stores line the streets and men push racks of clothes in and out of warehouses. This was a seamy neighbourhood of music halls and bordellos until the opening of **Macy's** department store (*page 82*) on Herald Square in 1901.

Madison Square Garden (*7th Ave at 32nd St; guided tours from 1000–1400 daily*) is a vast concert and sports arena built over the underground Pennsylvania Station. The destruction of the original Beaux Arts station building to make way for the arena in 1968 proved the catalyst for the successful campaign to preserve other New York landmarks. The **General Post Office** on 8th Avenue, designed by the same firm of architects to complement the station, gives a clue to the original style. Across the façade is a quotation from Herodotus, paying tribute to the postal service of the Persian empire: 'Neither snow nor rain nor heat nor gloom of night stays these couriers from the swift completion of their appointed rounds.' The Post Office is due to be incorporated into a renewed Penn Station concourse, a small atonement for the vandalism of the 1960s.

Chelsea Piers

23rd St and Hudson River. Tel: 212–336–6666. www.chelseapiers.com
Subway: C, E, 1, 9 to 23rd St. Bus: M1, M15, M22.

GIs sailed to war from these piers, immigrants stepped ashore and the Titanic would have docked here if she had not sunk on the way – but until 1995 this stretch of the **Hudson River** was better known as an open-air cruising spot. The transformation of four rusting jetties into a 30-acre sports village is one of the most visible signs yet of the changes sweeping New York. There are basketball courts, skating rinks, climbing walls and a pool, plus an indoor running track and a golf driving range facing the New Jersey shore. Less sporty types can relax with a harbour cruise or a drink in the brewpub beside the marina.

> **"** It is hard to imagine a busier place than a New York gym. It has all the passion, fury and groaning of the trading floor, with even more sweat. **"**
>
> **Joanna Coles, *The Times*, 1988**

Empire State Building

It may have been surpassed in height by the World Trade Center for a time, but the Empire State remains far and away the most evocative symbol of the New York skyline. Conceived during the skyscraper boom of the late 1920s, when the race was on to create the world's tallest building, the contracts were signed just weeks before the Wall Street crash. Despite this, the building was completed in just 410 days at the rate of four storeys a week – but when it opened in 1931 the space was so hard to let that it ended up being dubbed the 'Empty State Building'.

Constructed of granite and limestone and trimmed with stainless steel, the Empire State stood 1250 ft high before the addition of a TV tower added a further 200 ft. The original plans ended at the 86th floor, but a last-minute decision was made to add a zeppelin mooring mast – airships at that time being considered the transport of the future. Cynics suggest that the extra height was merely designed to put off rivals. After all, without the mast, the Empire State would only have surpassed the **Chrysler Building** – completed the previous year – by a few feet. And without the mast, **King Kong** would have had nothing to cling to as he met his death grappling with passing planes in the Empire State's most memorable movie scene.

> **"** *Oh Mighty City of New York! You are wonderful to behold,*
> *Your buildings are magnificent, the truth be it told,*
> *They were the only thing that seemed to arrest my eye,*
> *Because many of them are thirteen storeys high.* **"**

William McGonagall

From the outside, the first impression is of sheer verticality, as if all that mattered was the height. Look again and you notice that the building consists of ten elegantly tiered steps, designed to comply with the planning laws that required skyscrapers not to block out the light. Step inside the Art Deco entrance lobby on **Fifth Avenue**, lined with marble and adorned with a bas-relief image of the building. Then do what you have come here for – head for the top.

You can walk if you really want to – **a race** is held each February up the 1575 steps, with the winner usually reaching the 86th floor in around 11 minutes. Most people settle for the elevator, which whisks you up in less than a minute. From the observation deck and the outside walkway, Manhattan is spread beneath you; on clear days you can gaze far out into the Atlantic.

Queue again for the **lift to the observatory** on the 102nd floor. This is set into the tower, which lights up at night according to the colours of the season. On Valentine's Day it turns red; on St. Patrick's Day, green; on Independence Day it is red, white and blue. The lights are turned off during the spring and autumn migrations to prevent birds from crashing into the building.

The best time to come here is at dusk, to see the skyline by day and again as it lights up for the night. The queues can be long, so allow at least an hour for your visit.

> " I haven't the remotest idea what New York means by dubbing itself the Empire State. As far as I am aware, New York's many undoubted glories do not include overseas possessions. "
>
> **Bill Bryson, _Notes from a Big Country_, 1998**

Getting there:
350 5th Ave at 34th St.
Subway: B, D, F, N, Q, R to
34th St. Tel: 212–736–3100.
www.esbnyc.com
Open: 0930–2400 daily.
*Admission: **.*

Flatiron Building

Broadway and 5th Ave. Subway: F, N, R, 6 to 23rd St.

Looking down on the Flatiron Building from the top of the Empire State, it is hard to believe that this was once the tallest building in the world. Designed by Daniel Burnham, the pioneer of the skyscraper in Chicago, it caused a sensation when it went up in 1902. This was not just because of its height (300 ft) but also its extraordinary triangular shape, taking advantage of the street intersection between **Broadway**, **Fifth Avenue** and **23rd Street**. Some people predicted that strong winds would tear the building down; in fact, its shape had the unexpected effect of creating extra currents on the street, giving rise to regular gatherings of Peeping Toms hoping for a glimpse of female flesh. The view of the Flatiron from its northern end, where it narrows to a curve of just 6 ft, has inspired much lyrical photography and prose. Some writers compare it to an ocean liner sailing up Broadway; others to a flat iron, hence the name. Across the street, **Madison Square** is a pleasant park, lined with statues and full of office workers at lunchtime. This was the site of the original Madison Square Garden entertainment centre.

Gramercy Park

Subway: 6 to 23rd St.

Manhattan's only private park is open to the public for one day a year but otherwise only the residents of the square have keys. This charming square of **Italianate and Greek Revival houses** was laid out by Samuel Ruggles in the 1830s on the site of a former swamp. Designed to imitate the fashionable

London squares of the time, it later developed a reputation as an American Bloomsbury, home to writers and intellectuals including Edith Wharton, Herman Melville, Eugene O'Neill and Samuel Morse. O Henry wrote *Gift of the Magi* in a nearby tavern, and Stanford White, architect of the Washington Square arch and Pennsylvania Station, built himself the house which is now Gramercy Park Hotel.

Little Church Around the Corner

1 E 29th St. Subway: N, R, 6 to 28th St.

This Episcopal church, officially the **Church of the Transfiguration**, owes its nickname to an incident in 1870 when one Joseph Jefferson was trying to arrange the funeral of his friend George Holland, an actor. The pastor of the nearby Marble Collegiate Church refused – actors were regarded as the lowest of the low – and suggested Jefferson try 'the little church around the corner'. 'Then God bless the little church around the corner', he replied, and the name has stuck. The church's relationship with the theatre continues to this day.

Union Square

Subway: L, N, 4, 5, 6 to 14th St–Union Sq. Market: Mon, Wed, Fri, Sat 0800–1800.

In the 1970s this was a seedy haunt of drug-pushers; now it has been cleaned up and revitalised as the city's largest open-air produce market. New York's Greenmarkets were begun in 1976 as a way of bringing city dwellers into direct contact with the region's farmers. Now, four days a week, the square is buzzing with stalls selling fresh fruit and vegetables, maple syrup, jellies, vinegars and home-baked bread. There are also a few craft stalls, but the emphasis is on fresh, local (and largely organic) produce. Thanks to the market, **Union Square** has become one of Manhattan's leading shopping districts, with branches of Barnes and Noble, Virgin and Toys R Us.

> **"** *New York City will be a great place if they ever finish it.* **"**
>
> **O Henry (1862–1910)**

Shopping

Macy's

34th St, between 6th and 7th Aves.
Open: Mon–Sat 1000–2030,
Sun 1100–1900.

If you only have time to visit one New York department store, this should be the one. Its two million square feet of floor space include four floors of designer clothing as well as shoes, furs and household goods. The Macyland giftshop on the 8th floor has children's T-shirts and a candy store; designer clothes for kids are sold one floor down. Don't forget the basement, with gourmet foods and an espresso and juice bar. For those in need of retail therapy, call **Macy's By Appointment** (*tel: 212–494–4181*) and a personal shopper will be waiting with a selection of clothes when you arrive.

Lower Fifth Avenue

A new Fashion Avenue has sprung up in SoFi (South of Flatiron), based on lower Fifth Avenue and Union Square. The British men's designer **Paul Smith** (*108 5th Ave*) has his American flagship here; **Armani, Banana Republic** and **J.Crew** are all near by. **Eileen Fisher** (*103 5th Ave*) features elegant, casual women's fashions, while **Daffy's** *(111 5th Ave*) has two floors of bargain basements offering discounted designer clothes. Union Square is superstore territory, with branches of **Barnes & Noble, Virgin** and **Toys R Us**.

Bargain hunting

The area around Macy's is a good place to pick up designer clothes at heavily discounted prices. Rummage through the clothes at **Conway** (*Broadway and 35th St*) and you will probably pick up some good deals. North of here, 7th Avenue is known as 'Fashion Avenue', where clothes racks whizz in and out of the Garment District showrooms. Most of the business here is wholesale but it is worth looking out for sample sales. Sixth Avenue, from 14th to 23rd Streets, is a bargain-hunters' paradise once known as 'Ladies Mile'. Try **Burlington Coat Factory** (*116 W 23rd St at 6th Ave*) for coats, suits and shirts; **Filene's Basement** (*620 6th Ave*) for designer clearance sales; and **Old Navy** (*604 6th Ave*) for discounted teenage fashions. **Loehmann's** (*106 7th Ave at 17th St*) is good for designer labels at knockdown prices. At weekends, visit the **antiques and flea markets** at 6th Avenue and 26th Street for jewellery, Americana and vintage fashions.

Restaurants and bars

Chelsea

Chelsea Bistro and Bar
358 W 23rd St. Tel: 212–727–2026. **.
For delicious Bistro classics, this romantic restaurant with a garden and fireplace is an old-fashioned charmer.

El Cid
322 W 15th St between 8th and 9th Aves. Tel: 212–929–9332. *.
Authentic Spanish tapas – garlic sweetbreads and seafood salad – are washed down with pitchers of sangria in this Little Spain hideaway near the trendy meatpacking district.

Empire Diner
210 10th Ave at 22nd St. Tel: 212–243–2736. **. Drag queens, pre- and post-clubbers and Chelsea Hotel literati all end up at this high camp 24-hour diner, whose chrome and steel Art Deco bar featured in the opening shots of *Manhattan.*

La Luncheonette
130 10th Ave at 18th St. Tel: 212–675–0342. **. This funky Parisian bistro serves great home cooking in a West Chelsea location near Chelsea Piers.

Molly's

For a genuine New York Irish bar, try this fireside pub near Gramercy Park, with creamy beer, sawdust-covered floors and a welcoming hearth in winter (287 3rd Ave).

Gramercy

The Coffee Shop
29 Union Sq W. Tel: 212–243–7969. *. Come here to spot self-conscious fashion models tucking into Brazilian cuisine in a 1950s diner setting. Great if you can put up with the noise, the smoke and the crowds.

Tabla
11 Madison Ave (at 25th St). Tel: 212–889–0667. ***.
East meets West with delicious food here. An Indian-accented menu with very subtle flavours.

Gramercy Tavern
42 E 20th St. Tel: 212–477–0777. ***. It's not easy to get a table here but the bar serves meals all day and does not need a reservation. The food is New American, the setting late 19th-century.

Pete's Tavern
129 E 18th St at Irving Pl. Tel: 212–473–7676. **. Going strong since 1864, Pete's is one of the oldest bars in New York. Come here for home-brewed beer, Italian pub grub and a heady dose of Gramercy literary history.

Union Square Café
21 E 16th St. Tel: 212–243–4020. ***. New York's hottest lunch date serves eclectic Italian–Californian cuisine. Given the quality, the prices are surprisingly modest.

Bookstores

*New Yorkers mourned the demise of many of their local bookstores when **Barnes & Noble** began expanding into Manhattan in the 1980s – then they discovered the pleasures of a shop where you can spill coffee over the magazines and linger for hours in an easy chair.*

Barnes and Noble are now everywhere; their superstores, like that in Union Square, have Starbucks cafés, children's storytelling sessions and author readings most nights. All are open until at least 2100 and some stay open till midnight. The Upper West Side store at Broadway and 82nd Street has become the unlikely venue for one of the hottest singles scenes in Manhattan. By contrast, **Barnes & Noble Jr** (*120 E 86th St at Lexington Ave*) is just for kids. If you don't like superstores, try some of these:

Gotham Book Mart

41 W 7th St.

'Wise men fish here' says the sign above the entrance to this store, which Woody Allen described as 'everyone's fantasy of the ideal bookshop'. This is a place for people who love books. The shelves are stacked with new and second-hand books, mostly literature, philosophy and art – but no cookbooks, guidebooks or children's books. Founded in 1920 by Frances Steloff, the shop quickly became a hangout for literary types including the **Gershwins**, **T S Eliot** and **Anaïs Nin**. Steloff defied the censors to import copies of *Lady Chatterley's Lover* from Paris after it had been banned in the United States.

Strand Book Store

828 Broadway at 12th St; also at South Street Seaport.

Come here first as most books are reduced, including half-price review copies hot off the press. There are eight miles of shelves and more books piled up on the floor. The basement has an excellent selection of books about **New York**.

Black Orchid

303 E 81st St.

This crowded mystery bookstore stocks hundreds of **out-of-print titles** not available elsewhere.

A Different Light

151 W 19th St.

New York's largest **gay and lesbian bookshop** is open till midnight and hosts regular poetry readings, film screenings and musical events.

On the sidewalk

Ex-mayor Giuliani's crackdown on sidewalk vendors has not affected Manhattan's second-hand bookstalls; under laws relating to freedom of cultural expression, no one can be prevented from selling books.

Midtown Manhattan

Midtown is quintessential Manhattan. The crowded sidewalks, the speeding taxis and the long, straight avenues hemmed in by skyscrapers capture all of the city's favourite images. This is where you can most feel the raw energy of Manhattan and the restless pace of the streets. After a morning in Midtown, you soon understand why New Yorkers would get bored living anywhere else.

MIDTOWN MANHATTAN

Midtown Manhattan

Getting there: Almost all of the subway lines pass through Midtown. Useful routes are the B, D, F, Q to 42nd St or Rockefeller Center; N, R, 1 ,2, 3, 7, 9 to 42nd St–Times Sq.; and 4, 5, 6, 7 to 42nd St–Grand Central. The S shuttle train connects Grand Central with Times Sq.

Tourist information is available at Times Square Visitors Center, 1560 Broadway (between 46th and 47th Sts). Open: daily 0800–2000.

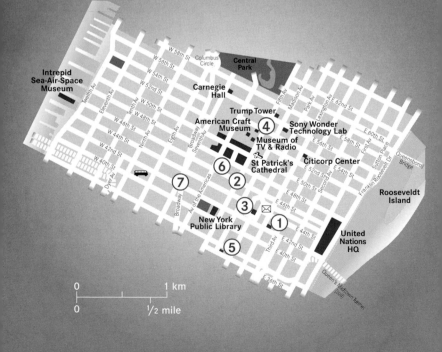

① Chrysler Building

The gleaming Art Deco spire with its motoring imagery is a distinctive feature of the Manhattan skyline and a tribute to the golden age of the motor car. For a few months in 1930 this was the tallest building on earth.
Pages 90–91

② Fifth Avenue

Theme stores specialising in basketball and Coca-Cola have recently challenged the dominance of the fashion houses in the most famous shopping street in Manhattan and possibly the world.
Pages 91, 106

③ Grand Central Terminal

The restoration of this Beaux Arts masterpiece is the single greatest triumph of the architectural preservation movement of the late 20th century.
Pages 92–93

④ Museum of Modern Art

Every major artist and movement of the 20th century, from Post-Impressionism to Pop Art, is represented in this outstanding collection, which also features photography, film, architecture and design. **Pages 94–95**

⑤ Morgan Library

The financier Pierpont Morgan commissioned this library to hold his collection of rare books, manuscripts and drawings. It is now open to the public as one of New York's most charming small museums. **Page 96**

⑥ Rockefeller Center

This 'city within a city', built during the 1930s, has become an enduring monument to a great New York philanthropist and a worldwide symbol of a New York Christmas .
Pages 98–99

⑦ Times Square

The neon lights of the 'Great White Way' sparkle at night in this heart of the Broadway theatre district, transformed in recent years from a sleazy strip to a place of safe family entertainment. **Pages 100–101**

Carnegie Hall

57th St and 7th Ave. Subway: N, R to 57th St; B, D, E to 7th Ave.
Tel: 212–903–9600. Guided tours: Mon, Tue, Thur, Fri 1130, 1400, 1500.

Financed by the steel magnate Andrew Carnegie, this was the first great concert hall in New York when it opened in 1891 with Tchaikovsky as guest conductor on the opening night. The former home of the **New York Philharmonic**, it was threatened with closure after the opening of the Lincoln Center in 1959 before being saved and restored to its original Renaissance splendour. The Beatles made their first New York appearance here in 1964 and it is still the venue that everyone wants to play. **Carnegie Hall Museum** (*1100–1630 daily except Wed; admission free*) has memorabilia of famous musicians, from Benny Goodman's clarinet to Arturo Toscanini's baton.

Chrysler Building

42nd St and Lexington Ave. Subway: 4, 5, 6, 7
to 42nd St–Grand Central. Tel: 212–682–3070.

This briefly became the world's tallest building when it was completed in 1930, a few months ahead of the Empire State. The architect, **William Van Alen**, had been engaged in a cat-and-mouse game with his rival, Craig Severance, who was working on the Bank of Manhattan in Wall Street. Severance had designed his building to be 2 ft higher than the Chrysler, but at the last minute Van Alen produced a spire, assembled in the fire shaft and pushed through the roof – thus guaranteeing his moment of glory. The owner, **Walter Chrysler**, wanted the building to symbolise his new motor company – hub caps were stuccoed to the walls and the stainless steel gargoyles were modelled on a Plymouth hood.

The glistening Art Deco spire, designed to resemble a radiator grill, is a much-loved symbol of the Manhattan skyline and a tribute to the futuristic dreams of the 1930s. During office hours, you can step inside **the lobby** – once a Chrysler showroom – with its Moroccan marble, Sienese limestone and elevators inlaid with walnut and ash.

Citicorp Center

53rd St and Lexington Ave. Subway: E, F to Lexington Ave; 6 to 51st St.

This sensational postmodern addition to the New York skyline was completed in 1978, with a tower built on stilts and a sloping roof designed to hold solar panels. The atrium inside the mall makes a pleasant place for lunch, but the most striking feature of the building is **St. Peter's Lutheran Church**, built into the base of the skyscraper. The granite exterior, symbolising the rock on which Christ built his church, contrasts sharply with the aluminium of the tower, and the sanctuary with its red oak pews is an oasis of calm.

Fifth Avenue

Subway: B, D, F, Q to Rockefeller Center; E, F to 5th Ave. See page 106 for shop listings.

Fifth Avenue runs all the way from Greenwich Village to Harlem, but to most people the name 'Fifth Avenue' conjures up the exclusive shopping stretch between Rockefeller Center and Central Park. From Saks to Tiffany's, all the great names of fashion are here, though corporate culture has begun to creep in with the arrival of Coca-Cola and Disney. Don't miss **Trump Tower** (*5th Ave and 57th St*), a splendidly flamboyant shopping mall and apartment block, with pink marble floors and a five-storey waterfall; like its creator Donald Trump, it is thought by many to symbolise the vulgar excesses of the 1980s. But as Trump said: 'If you're going to be thinking anyway, you might as well think big.'

" *When you see yourself as a New Yorker you talk faster, you walk faster and you think faster. "*

Ed Koch, Mayor of New York 1978–90

Grand Central Terminal

42nd St and Park Ave. Tel: 212–532–4900. Open: daily 0530–0130.
Subway: 4, 5, 6, 7 to 42nd St–Grand Central, or S shuttle from Times Sq.
Free walking tours, Wed 1230.

The story of the rebirth of Grand Central is a tale of good sense triumphing over greed – and of the changing attitudes towards the preservation of New York's architectural heritage. Built in 1913 on the site of an earlier Victorian station, the terminal is a classic example of the **Beaux Arts** school of design, which held that public buildings should be beautiful as well as functional, graceful in proportion yet massive in scale. The southern façade is dominated by a huge clock, surrounded by figures of classical gods; the marble staircase is modelled on the **Paris Opera**; the concourse, the size of a cathedral, has a ceiling painted with a vision of the night sky.

In the 1930s, the railroad conjured up romantic images; New York was the gateway to America, and passengers boarding the *Twentieth Century* to Chicago each evening would have the red carpet laid out. But as cars replaced trains and the terminal became a subway station, **Grand Central** gradually fell into decline. In 1965 its owners, Penn Central Railroad, proposed building a 55-storey skyscraper on top, although the station had already been declared an historic landmark; when permission was refused, they succeeded in having the Landmarks Law declared unconstitutional.

Memories were still fresh of the demolition of Pennsylvania Station, another Beaux Arts masterpiece whose demise had been much mourned. The former First Lady **Jacqueline Kennedy Onassis** threw herself into a campaign to save Grand Central from a similar fate. In 1978 the Supreme Court reversed the earlier decision, but the battle was only partly won. By then the station had become run-down and dangerous, a covered version of Times Square with its billboards, pickpockets and betting shops. The new owners decided that preservation was not enough; restoration was needed as well. The architect **John Belle** was commissioned to return the station to its glory days.

The new Grand Central Terminal was unveiled in 1998, with its polished marble, gold-plated chandeliers and the famous brass clock at its centre. The celebrated **Oyster Bar** (*page 107*) is still in the basement, but it has been joined by dozens of upmarket restaurants and shops. Grand Central is finally returning to its place at the heart of New York – and the constellations on the ceiling are shining once more.

Intrepid Sea–Air–Space Museum

Pier 86 (W 46th St. and 12th Ave). Tel: 212–245–0072. Subway to 42nd St then bus M42, or subway to 49th/50th St then bus M50. www.intrepid-museum.com. Open: Apr–Sept, Mon–Fri 1000–1700, Sat–Sun 1000–1900; Oct–Mar, Tue–Sun 1000–1700. Admission: ***.

The aircraft carrier *Intrepid* dominates the Hudson River waterfront and for anyone interested in military history it is well worth the trek to get there. A veteran of World War II and the Vietnam War, *Intrepid* survived seven bombs and five kamikaze attacks before being taken out of commission in 1974. The **flight deck** contains a collection of planes, including an A-12 Blackbird (the world's fastest spy plane) and a Polish Mig-21. Visitors can climb aboard the submarine *Growler* and the destroyer *Edson*, and see Sikorsky helicopters and captured Iraqi tanks. Some of the guides are ex-servicemen, who help to bring the exhibits to life. Near here, at Pier 83, is the departure point for the Circle Line cruises.

" *All of everything is concentrated here, population, theater, art, writing, publishing, importing, business, murder, mugging, luxury, poverty. It's all of everything. It goes all night. It is tireless and its air is charged with energy.* "

John Steinbeck (1902–68)

Museum of Modern Art

Now that it has become such a respected institution, it seems strange to remember that when MoMA opened in 1929 it was thought by many to be pushing the frontiers of art beyond acceptable boundaries. Then, Cubism and Surrealism were revolutionary concepts; these days in Manhattan, they seem positively conservative.

As with so much else in New York, the original inspiration came from a Rockefeller. Abby Aldrich Rockefeller had acquired a taste for modern art during her travels in Europe and persuaded her husband, John D Rockefeller Jr, to donate the land for a museum. What began with eight prints and a drawing has grown to become the world's foremost collection of modern art, spanning every period and style in Europe and America from the late 19th century onwards.

The core of the collection, on the second and third floors, is arranged in **chronological order**. The first three galleries are devoted to Post-Impressionism; masterpieces include *The Bather* by Cézanne, *The Sleeping Gypsy* by Rousseau and *The Starry Night* by Van Gogh. The next gallery contains *Les Demoiselles d'Avignon*, Picasso's monumental study of five Barcelona prostitutes. **Cubism** is well represented in Gallery 5, while Gallery 10 is devoted to the paintings of Piet Mondrian, whose *Broadway Boogie Woogie* evokes both Manhattan's grid system and the jazz age. The **Matisse** collection in Gallery 12 is dominated by *Dance*, a portrait of five female nudes thought to have been inspired by a group of Catalan fishermen dancing on the beach. Galleries 15 and 16, devoted to **Surrealism**, feature works by Miró and Magritte as well as Salvador Dali's desolate and mysterious *The Persistence of Memory*. A separate gallery on the second floor contains

> " *New York is something awful, something monstrous. I like to walk the streets, lost, but I recognize that New York is the world's great lie. New York is Senegal with machines.* "
>
> **Federico García Lorca (1898–1936)**

Monet's triptych *Water Lilies*, one of a series of studies of his garden at Giverny in Normandy, France.

The third floor features post-1940 painting and sculpture, with a particularly strong collection of American avant-garde and **Abstract Expressionist** art. Artists represented here include Jackson Pollock, Edward Hopper, Mark Rothko, Jasper Johns and Georgia O'Keeffe. In Gallery 20, Andrew Wyeth's *Christina's World* is a powerful study of a polio victim. The permanent collection concludes in Gallery 26 with masterpieces of **Abstract and Pop Art**, including Andy Warhol's *Gold Marilyn Monroe* and Roy Lichtenstein's *Drowning Girl*.

It was MoMA that pioneered the acceptance of contemporary art forms other than painting and sculpture, and the fourth floor **architecture and design collection** contains mass-

produced household and industrial objects including vacuum cleaners, Tiffany lamps and a Cisitalia GT car. There is also a large photography collection, and daily film and video screenings.

The **Abby Aldrich Rockefeller Sculpture Garden** on the ground floor makes a peaceful place to relax. There are works here by Giacometti, Moore and Rodin as well as Gaston Lachaise's *Standing Woman*, once condemned as grotesque and obscene but now regarded as an icon of sensual femininity. A door from the Sculpture Garden leads into the **Garden Café**, where free jazz concerts are held during the pay-what-you-wish Friday evening sessions. In July and August these are replaced by musical evenings in the garden itself.

Getting there: 11 W 53rd St. Tel: 212–708–9400.
Subway: E, F to 5th Ave. www.moma.org. Open: Thur and
Sat–Tue 1030–1745, Fri 1030–2015. Admission: ***
(Fri 1630–2015, pay what you wish).

Morgan Library

29 E 36th St at Madison Ave. Tel: 212–685–0008. Subway: 6 to 33rd St.
Open: Tue–Fri 1030–1700, Sat 1030–1800, Sun 1200–1800.
Guided tours: Tue–Fri 1430. Admission: **.

The financier J Pierpont Morgan (1837–1913) collected rare books like others collected Old Masters and in 1902 he commissioned Charles McKim to design 'a little museum building' for his collection. The resulting library, in the style of an Italian palace, is considered New York's supreme example of American Renaissance architecture.

The library and its collection were given to the American public in 1924 by Morgan's son, J P Morgan Jr. This is New York's most charming small museum, full of unexpected pleasures. The **West Room**, used by Pierpont Morgan as his study, is extravagantly furnished with ancient Greek and Babylonian sculptures and a carved ceiling imported from Florence. The **East Room**, where his library was kept, is stacked floor to ceiling with bookshelves. There are three Gutenberg Bibles, the 9th-century Lindau Gospels and a first folio edition of Shakespeare's plays.

The collection of early children's books includes a 1695 edition of *Tales of Mother Goose*. There are autographed manuscripts of Milton's *Paradise Lost* and Dickens' *A Christmas Carol*, original scores by Beethoven, Brahms and Mozart, and letters signed by George Washington, Napoléon and Queen Elizabeth I. Only a small selection is on display at any one time, but such is the scope of the collection that whatever you see is likely to be fascinating.

The library is connected to **Morgan House**, a brownstone mansion built for J P Morgan Jr which now contains an excellent bookshop. Between the two, the skylit Garden Court café makes a delightful setting for concerts and poetry readings on Friday evenings.

New York Public Library

*5th Ave and 42nd St. Tel: 212–869–8089. Subway: B, D, F, Q to 42nd St;
4, 5, 6 to 42nd St.–Grand Central; 7 to 5th Ave. www.nypl.org. Open:
Mon–Sat 1000–1800. Guided tours: Mon–Sat 1100, 1400. Admission free.*

The flight of stone steps on Fifth Avenue flanked by a pair of marble lions may be better known as the setting for the opening sequence of *Ghostbusters*, but beyond it stands one of the finest Beaux Arts buildings in Manhattan. The **New York Public Library**, completed in 1911 at a cost of £29 million, was hailed by the *New York Herald* on its opening day as 'a splendid temple of the mind'. The marble lobby, inscribed with the names of benefactors, lists all the great New York philanthropists; the result is a building which is 'to be maintained forever as a free library for the use of the people'.

The library's **collection** is staggering – more than 50 million items, from ancient Japanese scrolls to baseball cards and movie posters. A few of the items are on display in the **Gottesman exhibition hall**, but if time is limited head for the **Main Reading Room**, with its bronze reading lamps, ornate ceiling and arched windows flooded with light. Below here, the books are stored on 88 miles of shelves. Call slips are still sent down to the basement in cylinders and books are still sent up in pneumatic tubes, but time is catching up with the library. After a recent renovation, you can now just sit at your computer and access the library's collections on-line.

> " *Speaking of New York as a traveller, I have two faults to find with it. In the first place, there is nothing to see; and, in the second place, there is no mode of getting about.* "
>
> **Anthony Trollope (1815–82)**

Rockefeller Center

Subway: B, D, F, Q to Rockefeller Center.

This ambitious 'city within a city' is New York's supreme example of urban planning and a living museum of Art Deco architecture. Built during the 1930s, it began as a plan to move the Metropolitan Opera midtown; when that project fell through, John D Rockefeller Jr decided instead to transform the area into a commercial and entertainment complex, which remains the largest private building enterprise ever undertaken.

There are 14 buildings in all, connected by hidden underground passageways that manage to link offices, shops and a subway station. The best place to start is on **Fifth Avenue**, walking down the Promenade with the GE Building (at 850 ft, the tallest in the complex) ahead of you. This is one of the few genuine vistas in Manhattan; elsewhere in the city, it is rarely possible to step back far enough from a skyscraper to see it. At the end of the Promenade, inscribed on a granite block, is Rockefeller's personal credo, an eloquent statement of New York's democratic capitalist ethos. Beneath here, the sunken plaza at the heart of the Center acts as an **open-air café** in summer and a **skating rink** in winter. The lighting of the Christmas tree here each December is a popular New York spectacle that sets the scene for some of the most iconic images of Manhattan.

To explore the complex in more detail, pop into the lobby of the **GE Building** to pick up a free guide. This is particularly useful if you want to appreciate some of the Art Deco mosaics and sculpture that are incorporated into the buildings. Don't miss **Radio City Music Hall** (*6th Ave and 50th St; guided tours 1000–1700; admission ****), New York's largest theatre with 6000 seats and extravagant Art Deco furnishings. After a $70 million restoration in 1999, Radio City once again looks as awesome as intended when first built in 1932. This is the home of the Rockettes Christmas Spectacular, when the high-kicking chorus girls are joined by genuine camels and reindeer. You can learn all about it, and meet a Rockette, on one of the fascinating backstage tours.

St. Patrick's Cathedral

5th Ave and 50th St.

Tel: 212–753–2261. Subway: E, F to 5th Ave; 6 to 51st St. Open: daily 0700–2100. Admission free.

The largest Catholic church in the USA was completed in European Gothic style in 1879. It was built beyond the then city limits, but this turned out to be a shrewd move – the cathedral now finds itself with a prime piece of real estate on a street where commercial rents are the highest in the world. Not that there are any plans to sell up. Note the heavy **bronze doors** of the main entrance on Fifth Avenue, adorned with statues of New York saints.

Sony Wonder Technology Lab

Madison Ave and 56th St. Subway: E, F to 5th Ave; 4, 5, 6 to 59th St. Open: Tue–Wed and Fri–Sat 1000–1800, Thur 1000–2000, Sun 1200–1800. Admission free.

❝ *I believe that the world owes no man a living but owes every man the opportunity to make a living.* **❞**
John D Rockefeller Jr (1876–1960)

OK, so this is little more than a marketing gimmick, but it's free, it's fascinating and kids love it. You can create your own soundtrack, edit a Billy Joel video, surf the Net and learn about the **history of technology** in four floors of multimedia fun and games. You 'log on' with a computer, which records your image and voice and prints out a certificate of achievement when you leave. Just the place to take the kids on a rainy day.

Times Square

Times Square arouses strong feelings. To some it is a model of the new New York, a place where locals and tourists can enjoy themselves free from the attentions of pickpockets, pushers and prostitutes. To others it is a place that has lost its soul. When you hear critics moaning about the 'Disneyfication' of New York, you can be sure that they are talking about Times Square.

" *There is something about a Harlem blues club, or a Russian emigré café on Brighton Beach, that simply cannot be matched by a trip to the Walt Disney souvenir shop or one of the proliferation of themed burger bars feeding tourists in Manhattan.* "

Charles Laurence, *The Daily Telegraph*, 1998

Times Square is both admired and vilified because it is a living symbol of the changes taking place in New York. By the 1980s, the area around Times Square had become a sleazy hotchpotch of peep shows, strip joints and porn shops, where visitors coming out of Broadway theatres were hustled by dealers and prostitutes of uncertain gender. Today the area has been totally turned around. Much of the credit is due to the **Times Square Business Improvement District**, a consortium of local traders formed in 1992. Unarmed security officers clear the streets of 'quality-of-life' offenders; sanitation crews keep the area free of litter. High-profile businesses have been attracted, encouraged by the new, tourist-friendly image.

The subway station has been given a facelift. A new **Visitors Center** has been opened. Handsome art nouveau theatres have been restored. Most people agree that the changes have been for the better, but at the same time Times Square has lost some of its character. The days when Damon Runyon could describe a street cast of 'burlesque dolls and hoofers, saxophone players and midgets' have been replaced by a predictable cityscape of theme restaurants and shops. The greatest threats to your wallet these days come from **Warner Brothers** and the **Virgin Megastore**.

Not that Times Square has entirely lost its power to excite. The huge, neon-lit advertising signs, which led to Broadway being dubbed the 'Great White Way', still tower over the square at night, a symbol of New York recognised across the world. The electronic news bulletin which circles **Times Tower**, the first in the world when it broadcast the election results in 1928, still flashes out the latest news. Times Tower itself, once the offices of the *New York Times* from which Times Square takes its name, is still surrounded by revellers on New Year's Eve waiting for the famous 'big apple' to drop. This is one occasion when you would still be advised to keep an eye on your pockets.

Facing Times Tower across Broadway, the world's first **eco-skyscraper** – built entirely of recycled steel – is a symbol of the area's regeneration. Another is the **New Amsterdam Theater** on 42nd Street. Built in 1903 as one of the finest art nouveau theatres in America and for many years home to the Ziegfeld Follies, it later became a movie house and closed in 1985. After years of neglect, the building was bought by Disney, restored to its original splendour and reopened in 1997. Across the street, the **New Victory** became Broadway's first dedicated theatre for kids when it opened in 1995.

To escape the bustle of Times Square, head for **Bryant Park**. In the 1980s this was Manhattan's worst drug-dealing spot; now it is a pleasant green area of sculptures and wrought-iron chairs, with outdoor cafés and afternoon concerts in summer.

Getting there: Subway: N, R, 1, 2, 3, 7, 9 to 42nd St–Times Sq; A, B, C, D, E, F, Q to 42nd St. Visitors Center: 1560 Broadway (open daily 0800–2000).

The United Nations Buildings

Although San Francisco and Philadelphia were both at one time under consideration, the United Nations could only really be in New York. This is, after all, a city of outsiders, a city which in Bernard Shaw's memorable phrase is 'halfway between America and the world'. Every language heard inside the General Assembly chamber can also be heard on Manhattan's streets.

It was John D Rockefeller Jr who secured the United Nations for New York when he purchased the 18-acre plot of land beside the East River for $8.5 million in 1947. The UN had been founded a couple of years earlier at the end of World War II but was still searching for a permanent home. The land was cleared of cattle, slaughterhouses and slum dwellings; the residents were rehoused elsewhere and work began on the vast complex of UN buildings. Dominating it all is the **Secretariat**, a sheer glass plinth rising above the river and containing the offices of the Secretary-General.

In 1945, the UN had just 51 members; now there are 185, their flags (from Afghanistan to Zimbabwe) lined up on UN Plaza. They meet each autumn in the **General Assembly**, where each country has a single vote and the seating plan is decided by lottery; although the meetings are open to observers, security considerations mean that it is often difficult to get in.

When the General Assembly is not meeting, you can see inside the chamber on one of the regular guided tours. The guides also take you to the **Security Council**, overlooked by a painting of a phoenix, donated by Norway and said to symbolise the nations of the world rising from the ashes of World War II. The Security Council, whose permanent members are the USA, Russia, Britain, France and China, is where the real decisions are made; its role is to end conflicts, whether through negotiation, sanctions, peacekeeping operations or ultimately armed force.

Further along the corridor, the **Economic and Social Council** is responsible for 80 per cent of the UN's budget, focusing on education, health care, human rights and sustainable development. This is where the UN has had some of its greatest successes, in areas such as literacy and vaccination campaigns; unfortunately its achievements in these areas are often limited by squabbles over funding. It comes as a shock to discover that the UN's total annual budget is about four per cent of that for New York City.

> " There is no nation that has not contributed something to Manhattan, if only a turn of phrase or a category of bun. "
>
> **Jan Morris,**
> *Manhattan*,
> 1979

Keep an eye out for the **gifts from the various member nations**, like the hand-carved ivory sculpture of the Kunming to Chengdu railway from China and the stunning Chernobyl tapestry, presented by Belarus. Alternatively, skip the guided tour and wander down to the sunny waterfront gardens, where there are several sculptures on the theme of world peace. One of the most notable, *Swords into Plowshares*, was a gift from the former Soviet Union; another came from the former Yugoslavia.

A final point to remember is that the UN is on **neutral territory** – in other words, it is not part of the United States. If you are one of those people who cannot resist the urge to prove that you have visited yet another 'country', pop down to the basement and send a postcard using UN stamps.

Getting there: 1st Ave at 46th St. Tel: 212–963–7713.
Subway: 4, 5, 6, 7 to 42nd St–Grand Central then bus M42.
*Open: daily 0915–1645. Admission: ** (for guided tours).*

American Craft Museum

40 W 53rd St. Tel: 212–956–3535. Open: Tue, Wed, Fri, Sun 1000–1800, Thu 1000–2000.

This is the showcase home of the American Crafts Council. Come here to see hand-made quilts, ceramics, glass, textiles, silver and wood craft that date from the 1900s to the present day. Founded in 1956, this museum reopened in 1987 in the three-storey atrium of an office building.

General Electric Building

570 Lexington Ave. Not open to the public.

In 1931 architects Cross & Cross were asked to design this skyscraper. The colours were chosen to blend and contrast with St. Bartholomew's Church next door. These two buildings look wonderful together and the GE building is a significant addition to the Manhattan skyline. It is an Art Deco masterpiece from its marble and chrome lobby to its magnificent crown.

General Post Office

421 8th Ave (between 32nd and 33rd Sts). Tel: 212–330–3601.

This monumental post office was built in 1914 and designed by McKim, Mean and White as a complement to the first Penn Station, which was subsequently demolished in the 1960s. The post office is open 24 hours a day.

IBM Building

590 Madison Ave. Tel: 212–745–5994. Garden plaza. Open: daily 0800–2200.

This 43-storey building was designed by Edward Barnes and completed in 1983. It is a sleek, prism-shaped building of grey-green polished granite. The garden plaza is a public atrium.

Madison Square Garden

2 Penn Plaza (at 33rd and 7th Ave). Tel: 212–465–6741. www.thegarden.com.

You have to be really lucky to obtain tickets to see the
Knicks or the Rangers play at this very dramatic arena.
Tickets for the New York Liberty women's basketball team
or college basketball are easier to come by. Visitors can take
a tour of the 20,000-seat arena.

Radio City Music Hall

1260 Ave of the Americas (6th Ave at 50th St). Tel: 212–307–1000.

Completed in 1932, Radio City is a tribute to the Rockefeller
family, and considered to be one of the wonders of
Manhattan. Restored in 1999, the great hall's awesome
beauty can be seen as it was originally conceived. Built as a
place for family entertainment, Radio City opened with
shows that included opera, ballet, comedy and acrobatics.

St. Thomas' Church

1 W 53rd St. Tel: 212–757–7013. Open: daily 0700–1800.

This church was built between 1909 and 1914 to replace an
earlier structure destroyed in a fire. It is a beautiful
limestone building in the French Gothic style.

Trump Tower

725 5th Ave. Tel: 212–832–2000.

This is an extremely expensive apartment and office tower
– with looks to match – above a lavish six-storey atrium
with exclusive shops and cafés. Designed in 1983, a symbol
of Donald Trump's immense wealth, it is typical of the
modern trend towards vertical shopping centres. Visit
Tiffany's next door, the prestigious jewellers founded in
1837.

Shopping

There are three main shopping areas in Midtown. **Times Square** has theme stores, souvenir shops and the world's largest music store, **Virgin Megastore**, which stays open late into the night. **Diamond Row**, on West 47th Street, is where 80 per cent of the US diamond trade takes place. And **Fifth Avenue** between 49th and 58th Streets is, quite simply, the world capital of fashion.

A walk up Fifth Avenue

Begin at **Saks Fifth Avenue**, facing the Rockefeller Center between 49th and 50th Streets. This is one of New York's most exclusive department stores, with designer boutiques, free beauty treatments and a personal shopping service. Two blocks north, **Gianni Versace** has Italian designer clothes for men, women and children. Passing **Cartier**, **Liz Claiborne** and **Banana Republic**, you reach **Brooks Brothers**, renowned for casual and conservative menswear. Nearby, **Testoni** and **Gucci** offer fine Italian leather, and **Fortunoff** has discount jewellery. **Takashimaya**, between 54th and 55th Streets, is an elegant Japanese-owned department store with tasteful home furnishings and a Japanese tea room in the basement.

After 55th Street, the 'mallification' of Fifth Avenue becomes clearer with the appearance of the **Disney Store** and **Coca-Cola 5th Avenue** – but this block also contains **Henri Bendel**, another upmarket department store. As you approach 57th Street, high fashion takes over, with branches of **Prada**, **Fendi** and **Tiffany & Co**. This world-renowned jeweller, where Audrey Hepburn had *Breakfast at Tiffany's*, sells diamonds, gold, silver and pearls as well as more affordable items like scarves. **Bergdorf Goodman**, between 57th and 58th Streets, has designer clothes for men and women in two separate department stores facing each other across the street. Finally, at 58th Street, you reach **FAO Schwarz**, America's best-known toy store. Once you allow your children in here they will never want to leave.

57th Street

For two blocks east from Fifth Avenue, 57th Street has some of the most exclusive shopping in Manhattan – this is the sort of place where you need an appointment just to get past the uniformed doorman. There are branches of **Chanel**, **Hermès**, **Prada** and **Louis Vuitton** as well as **Burberrys** for coats.

Restaurants

Bryant Park Grill
25 W 40th St. Tel: 212–840–6500. **. Outdoor seating and a lively bar scene make this a favourite spot for summer brunches and pre-Broadway dinners.

Carnegie Deli
7th Ave at 55th St. Tel: 212–757–2245. **. The oversized sandwiches here are a New York institution and the queues outside tend to be long. Come here for great pastrami and cheesecake, but not if you're on a diet.

Caviar Russe
Madison Ave between 54th and 55th Sts. Tel: 212–980–5908. ***. If you've just spent a fortune at Tiffany's, celebrate with champagne, caviar and cigars.

Grand Central Oyster Bar
Grand Central Terminal, 42nd St. Tel: 212–490–6650. **. The freshest seafood and 20 varieties of oyster are served in a barrel-vaulted hallway beneath Grand Central. Crowded, noisy and great fun, especially at the cheap lunchtime counter bar.

Michael Jordan's The Steak House NYC
Grand Central Terminal, 42nd St. Tel: 212–655–2300. ***. The Chicago Bulls' basketball player has opened his first restaurant on the balcony of Grand Central's concourse, with magical views of the constellation-strewn ceiling. A place to see stars in more ways than one.

Rainbow Room
30 Rockefeller Plaza. Tel: 212–632–5100. ***. Lobster thermidor and baked Alaska with views from the 65th floor of the GE Building. Everything here is 1930s, from Cole Porter on the dance floor to the high camp Art Deco surroundings. Book well ahead for the restaurant, or try the cocktail bar instead.

Vong
200 E 54th St. Tel: 212–486–9592. ***. The craze for fusion food in Manhattan is perfectly exemplified by this trendy Thai–French restaurant, where the foie gras comes sautéed with mango and ginger.

Theme restaurants

The area around West 57th Street has seen a takeover of theme restaurants, offering burgers and steaks along with the souvenir T-shirts. Most are open all hours and do not take reservations. Popular themeries include the **Hard Rock Café** (*221 W 57th St*), **Harley-Davidson Café** (*6th Ave at 56th St*), **Planet Hollywood** (*140 W 57th St*) and the horror-themed **Jekyll & Hyde Club** (*6th Ave at 57th St*). **Motown Café** (*104 W 57th St*) has soul food and occasional live music, while **Fashion Café** (*51 Rockefeller Plaza*), owned by a group of supermodels, has walls lined with fashion memorabilia.

Restaurant Row

For a pre-theatre dinner menu, visit Restaurant Row, where 24 restaurants are found in a single block on West 46th Street between 8th and 9th Avenues.

On and Off Broadway

Every actor dreams of playing on Broadway. The 'Great White Way' conjures up romantic images of the 1920s, of Cole Porter and George Gershwin and Damon Runyon's Guys and Dolls. *In fact, there are few theatres on Broadway itself – the term 'Broadway' refers to the area around Times Square between 41st and 53rd Streets. As for Off-Broadway and Off-Off-Broadway, these have very little to do with geography at all.*

Basically, a Broadway theatre means one with a capacity of more than 500 seats, showing big-name productions, mostly lavish musicals like *Chicago* and *Miss Saigon*. Off-Broadway theatre began in Greenwich Village but has spread out across the city; the capacity is 100 to 500, the atmosphere more intimate but equally professional. Off-Off-Broadway, meanwhile, is the 'fringe' – experimental productions in

MIDTOWN MANHATTAN

> **"** *Please do not purchase tickets from solicitors on the street.* **"**
>
> **Sign outside New Amsterdam Theater**

small theatres, many in the East Village. Not all shows are confined to a single category. The most talked-about Broadway hit of the 1990s, *Rent*, which deals with a group of young East Village artists coming to terms with homelessness, drugs and AIDS, began life as an Off-Off-Broadway production at the New York Theater Workshop.

You can find listings and reviews of current shows in *Time Out* or Sunday's *New York Times*. To get tickets for a Broadway show, contact **Ticketmaster** (*tel: 212–307–4100; www.ticketmaster.com*), call in at the **Times Square Visitors Center** or go directly to the box office of the relevant theatre. For cheap Broadway and Off-Broadway tickets, especially if you have an open mind about what you want to see, queue at one of the **TKTS discount booths** which offer reductions of between 25 and 50 per cent on the day of the show (*TKTS at Broadway and 47th Street: open Mon–Sat 1500–2000, Sun 1100–1900; also Wed, Sat 1000–1400 for matinees*).

Alternatively, ask the theatre directly about standby tickets or pick up the 'twofer' (two for the price of one) coupons which are sometimes available at tourist information offices and kiosks.

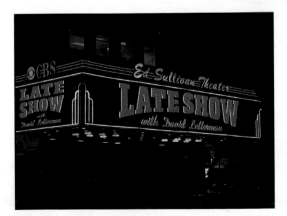

The Upper East Side

The money may be made on Wall Street, but it lives on the Upper East Side. Since the 1890s, when New York's high-society families began building their mock-European mansions on Fifth Avenue, the Upper East Side has meant status and wealth. Gloved doormen summon taxis to elegant apartments, and the city's finest museums are spread out along Museum Mile.

SEUM

MUSEUM CAFE

BEST OF

The Upper East Side

Getting there: Subway 6 runs beneath Lexington Ave, with stops between 59th and 103rd Sts. Buses M1, M2, M3 and M4 run up Madison Ave and down Fifth Ave along Museum Mile. Most museums, including the Met, are closed on Mondays, but check individual entries for details.

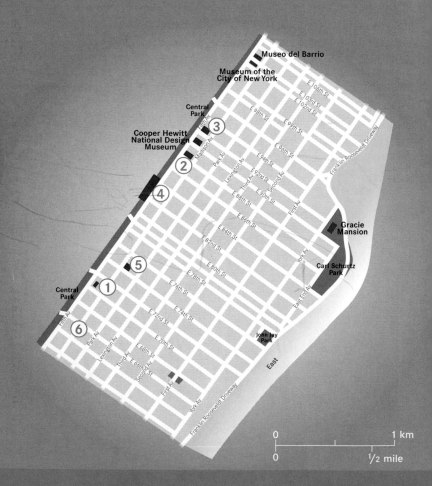

① Frick Collection

More like a private house than an art gallery, this collection of Old Masters and European furniture gives a rare glimpse into the lifestyle of a notorious 19th-century capitalist. **Page 115**

② Guggenheim Museum

Although it still has its critics, Frank Lloyd Wright's stunning architecture provides the perfect setting in which to view this eclectic collection of modern art. Matisse, Picasso and Warhol are all represented here. **Pages 116–117**

③ Jewish Museum

A thoughtful journey through the history of the Jewish people, from their roots in ancient Israel to the contemporary diaspora – including more than a million Jews living in New York. **Page 117**

④ Metropolitan Museum of Art

This is, quite simply, one of the great museums of the world. You could go in here knowing nothing about the history of Western art and thought, and come out an expert. **Pages 118–119**

⑤ Whitney Museum of American Art

This comprehensive collection of modern American art gives an insight into the lifestyle and cultural obsessions of 20th-century America. **Page 121**

⑥ Madison Avenue

With its upmarket shops, beauty salons and designer boutiques, Madison is like Fifth Avenue without the theme stores. **Page 124**

Cooper-Hewitt National Design Museum

E 91st St at 5th Ave. Tel: 212–849–8400. www.si.edu/ndm. Subway: 4, 5, 6 to 86th St. Open: Tue 1000–2100, Wed–Sat 1000–1700, Sun 1200–1700. Admission: ** (Tue 1800–2100, free).

When the steel magnate Andrew Carnegie decided to build 'the most modest, plainest and roomiest house in New York' in 1898, the Upper East Side was still a semi-rural area; soon everyone had to have an uptown mansion overlooking Central Park. In many respects Carnegie was ahead of his time – the house had central heating and primitive air-conditioning, and was the first private address in the city with its own elevator. In deference to his Scottish roots, the **Great Hall** was panelled in Scottish oak; the **Music Room** had crystal chandeliers and the **Garden Room** had leaded glass by Tiffany. All of this makes it an eminently suitable setting for the collection of the **National Design Museum**, begun by the three Hewitt sisters in 1897. The permanent collection contains everything from woodcuts to sand toys, but much of the space is given over to a changing series of temporary exhibitions.

> **❝** *New York is not a place in which to be poor or unsuccessful, although one has loads of company.* **❞**
>
> **Moss Hart (1904–61)**

Frick Collection

1 E 70th St. Tel: 212–288–0700. Subway: 6 to 68th St. www.frick.org. Open: Tue–Sat 1000–1800, Sun 1300–1800. Admission: **.

The industrialist Henry Clay Frick, one-time Chairman of Carnegie Steel, wanted to build a mansion that would not only hold his growing art collection but also put his rival and former partner in the shade. From an early age Frick had been interested in art – one employer reported that he worked hard but was 'a little too enthusiastic about pictures' – but as he grew older and richer he developed a taste for European Old Masters. His house and collection, left to the public on his death, have been preserved much as he enjoyed them, giving a fascinating insight into his lifestyle and tastes. There is fine French furniture, Limoges china and Renaissance bronzes, but the highlight is the **collection of paintings**. Among the works to look out for are Holbein's portrait of Sir Thomas More, El Greco's *St. Jerome*, a Rembrandt self-portrait and Velázquez' *King Philip IV of Spain*. There are also paintings by Titian, Bellini, Vermeer and Fragonard, and an extensive collection of English 18th-century portraits. Because it is largely the result of one man's tastes, the Frick Collection has a complete, unified feel which is lacking in some of the larger museums. As you relax in the **Garden Court**, contemplating the civilised lifestyle of a 19th-century capitalist, spare a thought for Frick's workers. The collector of Old Masters was known as a ruthless employer and notorious strike-breaker.

Gracie Mansion

East End Ave at 88th St. Subway: 4, 5, 6 to 86th St. Tel: 212–570–4751. Guided tours: Wed 1000–1400 by appointment. Admission: *.

Built in 1799 as the country estate of the shipping magnate Archibald Gracie, this has been the official home of the Mayor of New York since 1942 – despite the objections of the then Mayor, Fiorello La Guardia, who considered it far too opulent for his use. The clapboard house was restored in Federal style by Mayor Ed Koch in the 1980s and it is now possible to take a tour of its period rooms. Afterwards, stroll along the riverside promenade of the **Carl Schurz Park**, with its views of Hell Gate, where the East River meets Long Island Sound.

Guggenheim Museum

5th Ave at 89th St. Tel: 212–423–3500. www.guggenheim.org. Subway: 4, 5, 6 to 86th St. Open: Sun–Wed 0900–1800, Fri–Sat 0900–2000. Admission: *** (Fri 1800–2000, pay what you wish).

Robert Moses called it an 'inverted oatmeal dish'; the critic John Canaday described it as 'a war between architecture and painting in which both come out badly maimed'. Yet 40 years after it opened in 1959, New Yorkers are finally learning to love **Frank Lloyd Wright's** controversial structure. Designed as a spiral ramp coiling up to a skylit dome, from the outside it resembles a giant white shell. Wright – who died six months before the building was opened – always insisted that it represented an 'organic' style of architecture.

Solomon R Guggenheim started out as an itinerant pedlar and then made his fortune in mining. His artistic tastes were strictly conventional – like other millionaires of the time, he began by collecting **Old Masters** – until he came into contact with the European avant-garde. Influenced by his friend and adviser Baroness Hilla Rebay, whom he first met when he asked her to paint his portrait, he opened a

Museum of Non-Objective Painting and began to acquire works by artists such as Vasily Kandinsky and Paul Klee. In 1943 he commissioned Wright to design the new museum; he died six years later, leaving an endowment for the work to be completed.

Guggenheim's collection has grown over the years as a result of bequests and now covers everything from the Impressionist painters to Robert Mapplethorpe's photography. Ironically, many of the additions – considered masterpieces of modern art – would have been rejected by Guggenheim and Hilla Rebay as being too 'objective'. The items on display vary, but usually include works by Picasso, Van Gogh, Matisse, Chagall, Miró, Kandinsky and Alexander Calder. One striking modern addition is Francis Bacon's *Three Studies for a Crucifixion*; another is Andy Warhol's *Orange Disaster*. The best way to see it all is to take the elevator up to the top floor, then walk slowly down the ramp admiring the art and architecture at the same time. A number of new galleries were added in an extension to Wright's original building, completed in 1992.

Jewish Museum

*5th Ave at 92nd St. Tel: 212–423–3200. Subway: 4, 5 to 86th St; 6 to 96th St. Open: Sun–Mon, Wed–Thur 1100–1745, Tue 1100–2000. Admission: ** (Tue 1700–2000, pay what you wish).*

This eye-opening museum tells the story of the Jewish people throughout history using exhibits ranging from ancient ritual vessels to contemporary art. The permanent exhibition, on the third and fourth floors, shows how Jewish people have managed to adapt and diversify across the world while continuing to hold on to their fundamental traditions and beliefs. **Religious artefacts**, such as a 15th-century Torah ark from Italy and the mosaic wall of a 19th-century Persian synagogue, are mingled with interactive **computer displays** and the voices of contemporary Jews describing what their Jewishness means to them. George Segal's *Holocaust* sculpture, stark in its simplicity, shows a group of life-size plaster corpses with a single survivor standing behind a barbed-wire fence.

This museum is thoughtful, inspiring and beautifully laid out. Despite the serious subject matter, there is even something for children – an entertaining **children's gallery** on the fourth floor, with games and activities on the theme of Jewish festivals and traditions.

" *In New York, even if you're Catholic, you're Jewish.* **"**
Lenny Bruce

Metropolitan Museum of Art

The 'Met' is not like other museums. Many of its galleries would themselves be major museums elsewhere. It has world-class collections of African art, Renaissance sculpture, armour and musical instruments which few people manage to see. There is simply far too much for anyone to take in.

On a brief visit, you have to adopt survival strategies. Concentrate your energies on one section, then go back again the next day. Take a guided tour of the highlights, or attend one of the informative gallery talks. Give yourself breathing space to relax in one of the cafés or unwind in one of the many open spaces and courtyards. Or take the lift up to the roof garden, with its modern sculptures and views over Central Park.

One of the greatest pleasures of the Met is simply getting lost, stumbling across a Mexican monkey god here, a Flemish tapestry there. If you want to plan your visit, however, it is far more rewarding to explore one or two sections in detail than to attempt to cover the entire museum in a day. **The European Old Masters** alone, with more than a dozen Rembrandts and others by Botticelli, Tintoretto, Raphael, Titian, El Greco, Goya, Murillo, Velázquez, Bruegel and Rubens, take up 30 galleries. Another 21 rooms are devoted to **19th-century European art**, with entire galleries of Monet, Cézanne and Degas, paintings by Gauguin, Van Gogh, Renoir and Matisse and a Rodin sculpture gallery. Most people would agree that that was enough for one day.

The **American Wing** features Emanuel Leutze's *Washington Crossing the Delaware*, a supreme example of

Not only would it be impossible for anyone to walk round every item in a day; I don't believe it could be done on a bicycle.

Bernard Levin,
A Walk Up Fifth Avenue, 1989

romanticised patriotic art, as well as the pastoral 19th-century landscapes of the Hudson River School. Here too are John Singer Sargent's portraits of London society hostesses, including *Madame X*, which caused a storm when it was unveiled in Paris in 1884. The Garden Court is adorned with Louis Tiffany's stained glass and mosaics, and a series of American period rooms traces the development of interior design from the Colonial era, with its William and Mary furniture, to Frank Lloyd Wright's 'prairie house' in Minnesota.

The single most stunning exhibit is the **Temple of Dendur**, built on the banks of the Nile by the Roman emperor Augustus and moved to New York in 1963. The building of the first Aswan dam in 1900 caused the temple to be flooded every year, and the construction of the Aswan High Dam in 1960 would have submerged it altogether. In recognition of the American contribution towards preserving Nubia's ancient monuments, the Egyptian government presented the temple as a gift to the United States. It stands in its own purpose-built gallery overlooking Central Park, the centrepiece of a collection of Egyptian funerary art which is unmatched outside Cairo.

Another highlight is the collection of **Chinese art**, with Buddhist sculpture, Song dynasty paintings and a Ming-style scholar's garden, built in 1979 by craftsmen from Suzhou. If you have a week to spare, there is much, much more – Greek and Roman art, medieval art, Islamic art, Indian art, 20th-century painting.

To New Yorkers, the Met is more than a museum. Sunday brunch at the Met is a New York institution – while on Friday and Saturday evenings, Manhattan's dating scene shifts to the Balcony Bar, where a string quartet plays on a terrace overlooking the Great Hall.

Getting there: 5th Ave at 82nd St. Tel: 212–535–7710. Subway: 4, 5, 6 to 86th St. www.metmuseum.org. Open: Sun and Tue–Thur 0930–1730, Fri–Sat 0930–2100. Admission: suggested contribution.

Museo del Barrio

*5th Ave at 104th St. Tel: 212–831–7272. Subway: 6 to 103rd St.
www.elmuseo.org. Open: Wed–Sun 1100–1700. Admission: *.*

A quarter of all New Yorkers are of Hispanic descent and
many of them live in El Barrio, an area north of the Upper
East Side also known as Spanish Harlem. This museum, at
the top of Museum Mile, is an attempt to bridge the gap
between the formal approach of the other museums and
the vibrant **community culture** of El Barrio. Among the
exhibits are pre-Columbian artefacts and a collection of
santos de palo (carved wooden saints), but the museum also
showcases new work by contemporary Latin American
artists. It also features challenging displays on the life of
the community where salsa grew up among the *bodegas*
(grocery stores) and *casitas* (neighbourhood gardens).

Museum of the City of New York

*5th Ave at 103rd St. Tel: 212–534–1672. www.mcny.org. Subway: 6 to 103rd
St. Open: Wed–Sat 1000–1700, Sun 1200–1700. Admission: **.*

This museum, housed in a neo-Georgian Colonial mansion
overlooking Central Park, interprets the history of the
city through changing exhibitions. Among the items on

permanent display
are vintage fire
engines, antique
dolls' houses and
an exhibition on
the history of
Broadway. A
series of **period
rooms** shows
changing tastes in
furniture from the
Dutch Colonial
period through to
the early 20th
century, when the entrepreneurs of the so-called Gilded
Age attempted to decorate their homes in the grand
European style. The **Rockefeller Rooms** on the top floor

include the bedroom of John D Rockefeller Sr, designed in Japanese style in the 1880s and transferred to the museum when the Rockefeller house was destroyed to make room for the Museum of Modern Art. For a quick overview of New York history, see the *Big Apple* video on the ground floor.

Whitney Museum of American Art

945 Madison Ave at 75th St. www.whitney.org. Subway: 6 to 77th St. Open: Tue–Sun 1100–1800, Fri 1100–2100. Admission: *** (1800–2000 pay what you wish).

The sculptor and socialite Gertrude Vanderbilt Whitney (1877–1942) had a studio in Greenwich Village and used her enormous wealth to promote the careers of young American artists. When the Metropolitan Museum turned down her collection, she opened her own museum in 1931, specifically to bring the work of living artists to a wider audience.

In line with Whitney's original idea, most of the space is still devoted to **living artists** but the permanent galleries on the top floor contain the nucleus of her own collection. It was Whitney who sponsored Edward Hopper's first solo exhibition and his widow later left his entire collection of more than 2000 works to the museum. Hopper's paintings of solitary people and empty streets, such as *Early Sunday Morning*, create a stark sense of loneliness and isolation. Another gallery is devoted to **Georgia O'Keeffe**, best known for her abstract representations of nature. A third gallery exhibits the wire sculptures of Alexander Calder. His playful Circus features a big top, complete with acrobats, trapeze artists and clowns, and is accompanied by a video of Calder performing his circus act to a group of children.

The building was designed by **Marcel Breuer** in 1966 to have 'the vitality of the streets and the weight of a skyscraper'. Most people just see a brutal lump of concrete clad in grey granite.

" *I'd rather be a lamppost in New York than Mayor of Chicago.* "

Jimmy Walker, Mayor of New York 1926–32

Abigail Adams Smith Museum

*421 E 61st St (between 1st and York Aves). Tel: 212–838–6878. Guided tours available. **

This small museum sits well within earshot of FDR Drive and in the shadow of the Queensboro Bridge. There are nine richly-appointed period rooms. This federal-style structure was built in 1799 and is the only remaining building of its kind in Manhattan. The museum is named after Abigail Adams Smith, daughter of President John Adams, who built it originally as a 23-acre estate modelled after Mt Vernon. It was never completed.

Americas Society

680 Park Ave (at 68th St). Tel: 212–249–8950. Open Tue–Sun 1200–1800. Admission free.

Founded in 1967 by Nelson Rockefeller to heighten economic, social and cultural awareness of countries in the western hemisphere, the Americas Society features exhibitions, lectures and concerts. McKim, Mead and White designed this neo-Federal building in 1909.

American Society of Illustrators

128 E 63rd St (between Park and Lexington Aves). Tel: 212–838–2560. Admission free.

An interesting museum with different images of everyday things. The society has existed since 1901 to preserve the past and to promote the future of illustration. The museum's permanent collection includes work by Norman Rockwell and J C Lyendecker.

Asia Society

725 Park Ave (between 70th and 71st Sts). Tel: 212–517 ASIA.
www.asiasociety.org. Subway: 6 to 68th St. Open (with admission charge):
*Tue–Sat 1100–1800, Fri 1100–2000, Sun 1200–1700, free Fri 1800–2000. ***

This society was founded by John D Rockefeller III to encourage better relations between America and Asia and The Pacific. The society hosts many conferences, film shows and other cultural events. Galleries are open to the public and feature many exhibitions.

China Institute in America

125 E 65th St (between Park and Lexington Aves). Tel: 212–744–8181.
www.chinainstitute.org. Subway: 6 to 68th St. Open (with admission charge):
Mon, Wed, Fri–Sat: 1000–1700, Tue, Thu 1000–2000, Sun 1300–1700,
*free Tue, Thu 1800–2000. Gallery: ***

The Institute, housed in an elegant building, offers Chinese language classes, hosts lectures, films and discussions. You can also sign up for calligraphy and Chinese art classes. The Institute's gallery frequently hosts exhibitions of Chinese art.

Other buildings worth seeing are the **Metropolitan Club** (*1–11 E 60th St*), designed by Stanford White in the 1890's, the **Knickerbocker Club** (*2 E 62nd St*) and the **Lotos Club** (*5 E 66th St*). Other town houses and carriage houses line the streets of Park Ave, especially 69th St (between 3rd and Lexington) and in the Treadwell Farm Historic District on 61st and 62nd Sts (between 2nd and 3rd Aves).

Temple Emanu-El

1 E 65th St (at 5th Ave). Tel: 212–744–1400. Admission free.

This is said to house the largest Jewish congregation in the world. The impressive limestone, Moorish–Romanesque structure was completed in 1929 on the site of an Astor mansion and almost looks like a cathedral. The synagogue can seat 2500 people and has a beautiful bronze ark in the shape of a Sefer Torah. The temple regularly hosts recitals and concerts.

Shopping

*Madison Avenue in the 60s and 70s was a millionaires' playground, where film stars stepped out of beauty parlours and into boutiques on their way to sessions with their therapists. All the top designers have stores here, starting with Donna Karan's **DKNY** flagship (at 60th St). **Calvin Klein** is just across the road; as you head north, you come to **Giorgio Armani** (at 65th), **Dolce & Gabbana** (68th), **Gianfranco Ferre** (70th), **Yves St. Laurent** (70th) and **Ralph Lauren** (72nd).*

Barney's
660 Madison Ave at 61st St. Tel: 212–593–7800. The hippest of Manhattan's big department stores has eight floors of cutting-edge chic for uptown boys and girls.

Bloomingdales
3rd Ave at 59th St. Tel: 212–355–5900. The 'Metropolitan' of New York department stores was founded in 1872 and has gradually moved out of bargain basement territory into the sophisticated market. It's worth visiting Bloomie's once just to get one of their famous brown paper bags.

Boyd's
655 Madison Ave at 60th St. What started life as a pharmacy has grown into a celebrity hang-out offering manicures, makeovers and own-brand perfume. Come here to be pampered – at a price.

Julie's Artisan Gallery
687 Madison Ave at 67th St. In a street where fashion is all about the name on the label, Julie makes a case for fashion as work of art, with wacky hand-crafted designs for sweaters, jackets and jewellery.

Mackenzie & Childs
824 Madison Ave at 69th St. The very best of creative American design is on display at this whimsical store, where the attractions include a Victorian tree house. The best buy is the hand-painted pottery.

Shanghai Tang
667 Madison Ave at 61st St. Mao tunics, velvet jackets and silk dressing gowns are among the chic chinoiserie on sale at David Tang's sumptuous new department store.

Sherry-Lehmann
679 Madison Ave at 61st St. Tel: 212–838–7500. The top liquor store in Manhattan has a large range of American and imported wines, as well as whiskies, brandies and ports.

Restaurants

Barking Dog
3rd Ave at 94th St. Tel: 212–831–1800. *. This child-friendly diner with a canine theme has an all-day breakfast of pancakes and waffles, plus great milkshakes and more sophisticated dishes for grown-ups.

Daniel
60 E 65th St. Tel: 212–288–0033. ***. Celebrity chef Daniel Boulud has earned a reputation for his exceptional French cuisine. This is one of the hottest restaurants in Manhattan and you need to reserve well ahead.

Café Boulud
Surrey Hotel, 20 E 76th St (between 5th and Madison Aves). Tel: 212-772-2600. **.
In September 1998 Daniel Boulud opened Café Boulud, named after the gathering place his great-grandparents tended on their farm outside Lyon at the turn of the century. The contemporary Café Boulud is a French restaurant with an international accent and eclectic menu welcoming Manhattan's café society to a spot with the cosmopolitan chic of a Parisian rendezvous.

Mocca Hungarian
2nd Ave, between 82nd and 83rd Sts. Tel: 212–734–6470. No credit cards. *.
A throwback to the days when Yorkville was a Central European ghetto. Come here for huge portions of no-frills Hungarian cooking, from cheese pancakes to cherry soup.

Cello
53 E 77th St (between Madison and Park Ave). Tel: 212–517-1200. ***.
A magnificent, East Side, French seafood restaurant. The exquisite townhouse setting, smooth service and perfect meals leave you with a smile. Pre-fixe meals to choose from as well.

Serendipity
225 E 60th St (between 2nd and 3rd Aves). Tel: 212–838–3531. **. After shopping at Bloomie's, try this popular family restaurant, decked out like a doll's-house with velvet, lace and Tiffany lamps. The treat here is the dessert menu, from banana split to frozen hot chocolate.

Atlantic Grill
1341 3rd Ave (between 76th and 77th Sts). Tel: 212–988-9200. **.
Great seafood with spunk, this very popular and always busy restaurant is well worth a visit.

Afternoon tea

Take a break from your shopping with tea and scones in the rotunda of the Hotel Pierre (5th Ave at 61st St), an Art Deco landmark where Salvador Dalí used to stay. Other good hotels for afternoon tea are the Plaza (5th Ave at 59th St), Mayfair (Park Ave at 65th St), Carlyle (Madison Ave at 76th St) and Stanhope (5th Ave at 81st St).

New York's other museums

The great art collections may be found on Museum Mile, but New York has more than 120 museums covering everything from Tibetan art to the American piano. Some, like the **Ukrainian Museum** *(*page 51*), are devoted to the city's ethnic groups; others, like the* **Lower East Side Tenement Museum** *(*page 53*), to its social history. A visit to one of the smaller, specialist museums can often be just as rewarding as to the Guggenheim or the Met – they tend to be less crowded, cheaper and you can leave after an hour without feeling exhausted.*

" *New York City for a while had its own chocolate bar – called appropriately enough Nutty New Yorker – which wasn't too bad, although buying one was a bit disconcerting, like admitting you were in therapy or something.* **"**
Daniel Drennan, *The New York Diaries***, 1998**

American Irish Historical Society

991 Fifth Ave. (between 80th and 81st Sts). Tel: 212–288–2263.
www.aihs.org. (open to the public by appointment).

The society features a substantial library and a gallery in its 100-year-old building, which offers temporary exhibitions to highlight the Irish contributions to American Society. There are frequent readings, lectures and concerts.

Museum of American Financial History

28 Broadway. Tel: 212–908-4110. www.financialhistory.org. Subway: 4, 5 to
Bowling Green; Subway: 1, 9 to Rector St. Open: Mon–Fri 1130–1430.
Admission free.

Antique stock market equipment from the days before electronic trading is displayed in the lobby of John D Rockefeller's former headquarters. Come here after visiting the New York Stock Exchange to see how things have changed.

Museum of TV and Radio

23 W 52nd St. Tel: 212–621–6600. www.mtr.org. Subway: 1, 9 to 50th St;
6 to 51st St; E, F to 53rd St. Open: Tue–Wed and Sat–Sun 1200–1800,
Thur 1200–2000, Fri 1200–1800. Admission: **.

Choose from a computer catalogue of more than 50,000 TV and radio broadcasts then watch on your own private viewing console. A chance to relive one of the great moments of 20th-century history or rediscover a favourite childhood memory.

New York City Police Museum

100 Old Slip. Subway: 4, 5 Wall Street. Open Tue–Sun 1000–1800.
Tel: 212–480–3100. www.nycpolicemuseum.org.
Admission free (donations welcome).

Firearms, badges, uniforms and other police memorabilia are on display in the NYPD's police academy. The captured goods include counterfeit money, Al Capone's gun and a genuine machine gun concealed in a violin case. The museum has relocated to the headquarters of the city's first police precinct.

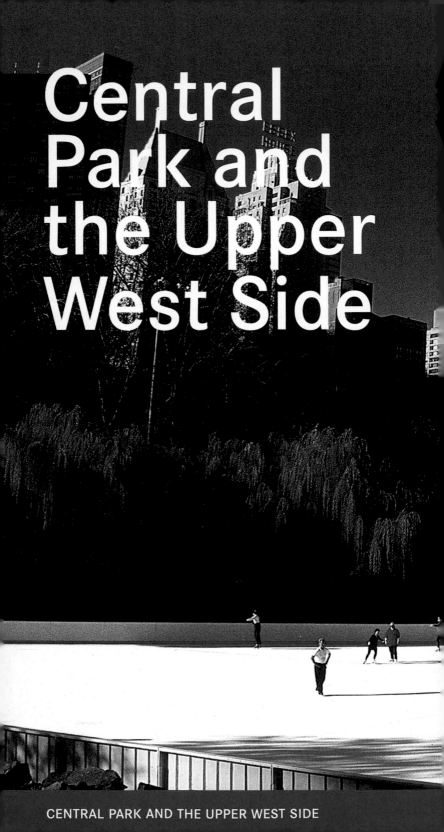

Central Park and the Upper West Side

With a tradition of liberal politics and a population of actors and writers, the Upper West Side is one of Manhattan's most relaxed neighbourhoods. An influx of young professionals has created a lively singles scene and given rise to the epithet 'yuppie west side', but this remains a genuine and diverse community with a laid-back, friendly feel – helped by the soothing presence of Central Park.

CENTRAL PARK AND THE UPPER WEST SIDE

Central Park and the Upper West Side

Getting there: **Subway:** *A, B, C, D, 1, 9 to 59th St–Columbus Circle; B, C to Central Park West between 72nd and 96th Sts; 1, 9 to 66th St–Lincoln Center and stops to 96th St.*

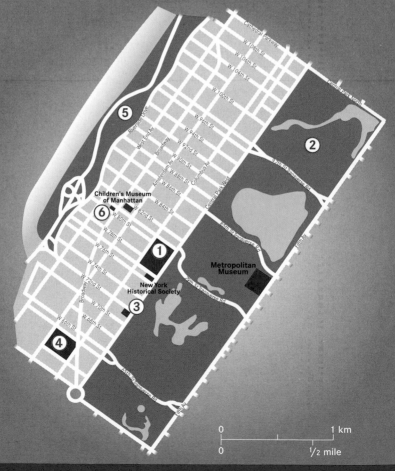

Children's Museum
of Manhattan

New York
Historical Society

Metropolitan
Museum

0   1 km

0   ½ mile

① American Museum of Natural History

The new Hall of Biodiversity adds a spectacular modern relevance to this museum charting the evolution of life on earth. The highlights include a collection of dinosaur fossils and a series of dioramas portraying animals in their natural habitats.
Pages 132–133

② Central Park

It is hard to imagine Manhattan without Central Park, a giant open-air playground which acts as the city's green lung – but if the original city planners had had their way, Central Park would not be here at all.
Pages 134–135, 138

③ Dakota Building

The name of New York's first luxury apartment block will forever be linked with that of John Lennon, who was killed outside the building in 1980. His widow, Yoko Ono, still lives here.
Page 136

④ Lincoln Center

The largest performing arts complex in the city, home to the Metropolitan Opera and the New York Philharmonic, was built in the 1960s on the streets where the Sharks and the Jets fought it out in *West Side Story*.
Pages 136–137, 139

⑤ Riverside Park

If Central Park overwhelms, this other park has a more genuine neighbourhood feel, with Westsiders walking their dogs and enjoying peaceful views over the Hudson River.
Page 137

⑥ Zabar's

The undisputed uptown gourmet mecca began life as a kosher deli in Brooklyn. Shoppers from all over Manhattan come here at weekends for smoked salmon, caviar, French cheeses and fresh bread.
Page 138

American Museum of Natural History

Founded in 1869 during the Darwinian era of discovery, the whole tone of this great museum belongs to an earlier age, when anthropology was just another branch of biology and the people of 'primitive' cultures were studied as if they were animals. These days, there is something unsettling about finding images of Yoruba deities lumped in with stuffed gorillas as examples of natural history. Not surprisingly, given its origins, the museum displays the mentality of the colonial explorer.

> **"** New York makes some think of the collapse of civilization, about Sodom and Gomorrah, the end of the world. The end wouldn't come as a surprise here. Many people already bank on it. **"**
>
> **Saul Bellow (born 1915)**

But put aside such modern thoughts, and the collections are stunning. Enter the museum from Central Park and the first thing you see is a 55-ft skeleton of a **Barosaurus dinosaur**. Like so many of the exhibits, it is hard to tell whether this is a genuine fossil or a work of art. In fact it is a replica, constructed out of fibreglass, but copied precisely from a 150-million-year-old skeleton that was discovered in the southwest USA.

The **fossil halls** on the fourth floor provide a journey through the history of evolution, from the earliest vertebrates (whales, turtles and fishes) to the forerunners of today's elephants and horses. Two of the galleries are devoted to dinosaurs, with complete skeletons of Apatosaurus and Tyrannosaurus Rex. Also here is an Oviraptor fossil sitting over a nest of eggs, discovered in the Gobi desert in 1993. The fossil, 72 million years old, gives the clearest proof yet of the evolutionary link between dinosaurs and birds.

You could easily spend all day here, but if time is short, take one of the free guided tours of the museum highlights, which leave every hour from the **Hall of African Mammals**. This hall, named after the explorer Carl Akeley, contains a group of elephants which he captured and stuffed himself, as well as giraffes, zebra and rhinoceros skilfully displayed in artistic representations of their natural habitats. There are similar lifelike dioramas of beavers, bears and wolves in the **Hall of North American Mammals**, and of leopards and tigers in the **Hall of Asian Mammals**.

Other highlights include the **Hall of Ocean Life**, where a 94-ft replica blue whale hangs from the ceiling; the Hall of Reptiles and Amphibians, with three Komodo dragons; the **Hall of Minerals and Gems**, containing the world's largest sapphire (briefly stolen in 1964) and other jewels valued at £80 million; and the **Hall of Meteorites**, with a 34-ton meteorite from Greenland and three rocks from the moon. **The Hall of Human Biology and Evolution** features a see-through hologram of the female body as well as dioramas portraying our ancient ancestors in their prehistoric habitats, while the new **Hall of Biodiversity** is a largely successful attempt to bring the museum up to date with a walk-through re-creation of a Central African rainforest and a video tour of the world's threatened ecosystems.

A new **Earth and Space Center**, containing a planetarium and a Big Bang Theater re-creating the first moments of the universe, has opened in 2000. In the meantime, the giant-screen Imax Theater has regular screenings of films on wildlife and cosmic themes.

Getting there: Central Park West at 79th St. Tel: 212–769–5100. Subway: B, C to 81st St; 1, 9 to 79th St. www.amnh.org. Open: Sun–Thur 1000–1745, Fri–Sat 1000–2045. Admission: **.

Central Park

When Woody Allen offered his 17-year-old date in Manhattan *the chance to do anything she wanted, she chose a night-time carriage ride around Central Park. To many New Yorkers, Central Park conjures up all that is magical and romantic about their city. This is where they come to walk, jog, cycle or skate, to get married, fall in love or simply to escape from the relentless summer humidity and the pressures of city life. Central Park is the place that restores New Yorkers to sanity.*

It is hard to imagine Manhattan without Central Park, but it very nearly didn't happen at all. The original grid plan did not allow for green space, and it was only after a lengthy campaign by William Cullen Bryant of the *New York Post* that the architects Olmsted and Vaux were commissioned in 1858 to design a park. An 843-acre rectangular plot of swampland and shanty town was levelled and turned into a pastoral, man-made landscape – which is why it fits so neatly into the Manhattan grid system.

Most of the action takes place in the southern section of the park, between 59th and 80th Streets. Start at the **Dairy** (*open Tue–Sun 1000–1700*), an information centre where you can pick up maps and details of events. Near here, the **Central Park Wildlife Conservation Center** (*open Mon–Fri 1000–1700, Sat–Sun 1030–1730; admission **) is a small zoo with penguins, snow monkeys and polar bears. Other nearby attractions include the **Wollman Skating Rink** and a charming **Carousel**, dating from 1908.

Rollerbladers do their tricks on **The Mall**, a canopy of elm trees lined with statues of famous authors and leading to the fountain at **Bethesda Terrace**. Near here, in the **Rumsey Playfield**, the Summerstage is a venue for free concerts and poetry readings. West of Bethesda Fountain, **Strawberry Fields** is a memorial garden to John Lennon, established by Yoko Ono and centred around an Italian mosaic featuring the single word *Imagine*. Across the park, kids sail remote-control model boats on **Conservatory Water**, where playful

statues of Alice in Wonderland and Hans Christian Andersen line the banks. If you see people with binoculars staring up at Woody Allen's apartment on Fifth Avenue, it's not Woody they're interested in but a pair of red-tailed hawks that have taken to nesting on the roof.

A register of bird sightings is kept at the **Boathouse**, where you can hire rowing-boats for trips on **The Lake**. Alternatively, walk across **Bow Bridge** (Manhattan's favourite kissing spot) and into **The Ramble**, a thickly wooded area once popular with the city's gays. This is a great place to get lost, but not after dark, when you should stick to the well-lit paths. A few high-profile murders and muggings have given Central Park a reputation for violent crime, and although the fears are exaggerated, the dangers are real enough.

> *If you should happen after dark To find yourself in Central Park Ignore the paths that beckon you And hurry, hurry to the zoo And creep into the tiger's lair Frankly, you'll be safer there.*

Ogden Nash, 1947

North of the Ramble, **Belvedere Castle** is the best lookout point in the park, with stunning views of the skyline as the sun dips behind the skyscrapers. Near here is the open-air **Delacorte Theater**, where free summer performances of Shakespeare are held; the **Shakespeare Garden**, with plants mentioned in Shakespeare's plays; and the **Swedish Cottage**, used for marionette shows. North of the **Great Lawn**, where the Metropolitan Opera give occasional free concerts in summer, the park grows wilder and less crowded. Look out for Madonna with her bodyguards jogging around the **Reservoir**, for wedding parties in the formal Conservatory Garden, and for Puerto Rican families fishing and swimming in **Harlem Meer** and the **Lasker Pool**.

See page 138 for further details of activities.

Children's Museum of Manhattan

The Tisch Building. 212 W 83rd St. Subway: 1, 9 to 86th St; B, C to 81st St. Tel: 212–721–1223. www.cmom.org. Open: Wed–Sun 1000–1700. Admission: **.

If your kids are getting bored with Manhattan, bring them to this stimulating museum where the emphasis is on learning through play. Four floors of hands-on activities include exhibitions on science, the environment and the human body, a TV studio where children can direct their own shows, and a creative play area for the under-fours. Call before you go for details of special events, such as storytelling workshops and performances of puppet theatre.

Dakota Building

Central Park West at 72nd St.

The Dakota was New York's first luxury apartment building when it opened in 1884 and the joke was that it was so far out west that it might as well be in Dakota. Before long, Central Park West (thought to be a more attractive name than 8th Avenue) was the city's most fashionable address and it has stayed that way ever since. Leonard Bernstein, Judy Garland and Boris Karloff have all lived in this Renaissance-style palace, and in 1969 it was the setting for the film *Rosemary's Baby*, whose star Mia Farrow lives near by.

Since 1980, the Dakota has been remembered as the place where John Lennon was shot dead. His widow, Yoko Ono, still lives in the building and maintains the Strawberry Fields memorial garden in Central Park (*page 135*).

Lincoln Center

Broadway and 64th St. Subway: 1, 9 to 66th St–Lincoln Center. Guided tours daily 1000–1700 (for reservations, tel: 212–875–5350).

New York's premier performance space was conceived in the 1960s as an ambitious project in urban renewal. With funds from the Rockefeller family, theatres and concert halls were brought together in a single complex on the site of what had been a notorious slum. The highlight is the **Metropolitan**

Opera House, with its plush velvet, African rosewood and glittering chandeliers; the foyer contains a pair of murals by Marc Chagall, but these are usually kept covered up to protect them from sunlight. Other buildings in the complex include the **New York State Theater** (home to the **New York City Ballet**) and **Avery Fisher Hall** (home to the **New York Philharmonic**). At the centre of it all is the **Lincoln Plaza**, with a fountain by Philip Johnson and a sculpture by Henry Moore.

New York Historical Society

77th St and Central Park West.
Tel: 212–873–3400. Subway: 1, 9
to 79th St; B, C to 81st St. Open: Tue–Sun
1100–1700. Admission: **.

New York's oldest museum was founded in 1804 to record the early history of the American republic. Among its treasures are Federal period furniture, landscapes of the Hudson River School, John James Audubon's original watercolours for *The Birds of America* and a portrait of the British governor, Lord Cornbury, in drag. Downstairs, at **Kid City**, children can build skyscrapers, dress up in period clothes and compare the Broadway of a century ago to today.

Riverside Park

Subway: 1, 9 to 79th St, 86th St, 96th St or 103rd St.

This long, narrow park, with a wide promenade and views over the Hudson River, is one of the most attractive spots in the city. A footpath from the park leads to the **79th Street Boat Basin**, where many of New York's houseboats are moored. Above the park, Riverside Drive is one of the most exclusive addresses in Manhattan, with elegant brownstone houses and European-style apartment blocks.

" *There are two things that really annoy me about New Yorkers. One is that they're always bragging about how they've got the biggest this, the best that. The other is that they're always right.* **"**

George Himes, Big Apple greeter on the Upper West Side, 1998

Central Park – activities and events

*Go rollerblading in summer and ice-skating in winter at the **Wollman Rink**, near the southern entrance to the park. This is particularly special at night, with the Midtown skyline as a backdrop.*

During the day you can also hire rollerblades and skates for getting around the park. Bikes can be rented from the **Boathouse**, along with rowing-boats, and horse riding is available at the **Claremont Stables** (*175 W 89th St; tel: 212–724–5100*). For a leisurely but expensive treat, take one of the **carriage rides** departing from the park's southeast corner or from the Tavern on the Green.

Keep a look out in summer for free events. **Shakespeare in the Park** is an annual festival at the Delacorte Theater; tickets are free at the box office from 1300 on the day of the show, and the queues tend to be long. The **Summerstage** has free outdoor concerts between June and August, and there is children's storytelling at 1100 each Saturday morning at the Hans Christian Andersen statue beside Conservatory Water. The **Metropolitan Opera** (*tel: 212–362–6000*) and **New York Philharmonic** (*tel: 212–875–5030*) both give free summer concerts on the Great Lawn which are well worth catching if you are there at the right time. Finally, not free but still good value, book tickets for one of the marionette shows at the **Swedish Cottage** (*tel: 212–988–9093*).

Shopping

Food lovers should head for Broadway between 74th and 81st Streets. **Fairway** may look like an ordinary supermarket but it has an excellent range of fresh produce as well as imported cheeses. **Citarella** is an upmarket fish store with a seafood and oyster bar and a full range of prepared meals. These are nothing, though, compared to **Zabar's** (*2245 Broadway at 80th St*). Sausages hang from the ceiling; salmon is sliced before your eyes; the smell of fresh coffee mingles with that of ripe cheese. Upstairs is devoted to every kind of kitchen equipment you ever imagined. **H&H**, on the same block, sells the best bagels in Manhattan.

> " *A Zabar's shopping bag is a recognized status symbol. It tells the world you're a cultivated and discriminating gourmet, instead of just another New York shlemiel buying a hot pastrami on rye and a sour pickle to go.* "
>
> **Helene Hanff,**
> *Apple Of My Eye*, 1977

Restaurants

Café des Artistes
67th St at Central Park West.
Tel: 212–877–3500. ***. The 1934
mural of cavorting nymphs sets the tone
for this romantic French restaurant and
cocktail bar. Be sure to leave some room
for the heavenly chocolate desserts.

Café Fiorello
1900 Broadway. Tel: 212–595–5330.
**. This bustling Italian eaterie
opposite the Lincoln Center plaza is a
good place to eat before or after the
show. The pasta is made fresh daily
and there is also a large antipasto bar.

Sarabeth's Kitchen
Hotel Wales, 1295 Madison Ave
(between 92nd and 93rd Sts).
Tel: 212–410–7335. **. Expect to
queue for Sunday brunch at this
popular homestyle eaterie, where the
choices include chicken, pancakes and
smoked salmon with scrambled eggs.

Shun Lee
43 W 65th St. Tel: 212–595–8895. **.
The top uptown Chinese restaurant is
well placed for the Lincoln Center,
with a *dim sum* café next door for
anyone in a hurry.

Tavern on the Green
Central Park West at 67th St.
Tel: 212–873–3200. ***. Hopelessly
romantic or unbelievably kitsch?
Whatever the answer, this place has
got it right as it serves more meals
than any other restaurant in the USA.
The rhinestone ceilings and crystal
chandeliers make this more like walking
into a fairy tale than a restaurant;
the horse-drawn carriages, and the
twinkling lights on the trees in winter,
only add to the effect. The food is
standard American, but then you don't
come here for the food.

Music at the Lincoln Center

Tickets for opera, classical music, ballet
and jazz are available from the box
office of the relevant theatre or from
Centercharge (*tel: 212–721–6500*).
Discounted tickets for some performances
(though not the Metropolitan Opera)
are sometimes also available on the day
of the show from the **TKTS booths**
on Broadway (*page 109*). The
world's leading opera singers perform
at the **Metropolitan Opera**
(*tel: 212–362–6000*) and the prices
reflect this; the **New York City Opera**
(*tel: 212–870–5570*) is more accessible.
The **New York Philharmonic**
(*tel: 212–875–5030*) has a policy of
selling cheap tickets for its open
rehearsals on Thursday mornings.

Look out too for free open-air concerts
in the plaza in summer and the **Big
Apple Circus** in Damrosch Park
between November and January.

The singles scene

Fuelled by an influx of young, single
professionals, the dating scene on
the Upper West Side is the hottest in
Manhattan. Try the café at **Barnes
& Noble** (*Broadway and 82nd St*),
where prospective partners eye each
other up over the magazines, or **Drip**
(*489 Amsterdam Ave*), a coffee bar
turned dating agency where you can
order a latte and a rice-crispie treat
and flick through biographies placed
in ring binders on the tables.

Crime, punishment and zero tolerance

Read this carefully in case you don't believe it – New York is one of America's safest cities. The FBI keeps league tables of violent crime and New York does not even make the first 100 places. Since 1990, the murder rate has dropped by more than 60 per cent to levels not seen since the 1960s. More significantly for tourists, 80 per cent of murder victims are known to their killers.

Rudolph Giuliani, the ex-Mayor from 1993 till 2001, has claimed much of the credit for the drop in crime, but a greater influence is probably William Bratton, the police commissioner forced out of office by Giuliani in 1996. It was Bratton who developed the 'broken window' theory of crime prevention, which has influenced police forces across America and Europe. By allowing estates to become run down, he argued, and failing to challenge vandalism, litter and graffiti, you contributed to the creation of no-go areas, which would become hotbeds for more serious crime. Instead, by adopting 'zero tolerance' of 'quality of life' crimes – begging, drunkenness, drugs, prostitution – you encouraged an atmosphere of public order in which the streets and subways felt safe. And as most crimes are committed by the same people, by arresting someone for jumping the turnstiles you may also catch a drug dealer with a handgun.

The results of this policy can be seen in the huge number of police on the streets – some 40,000 in all. Many people feel uneasy about this, but reluctantly admit that they feel more comfortable with a member of New York's Finest than a drug dealer on every corner. The police may be heavy-handed and occasionally corrupt, but they are also ruthlessly professional and most people feel reassured rather than threatened by their presence. Streets and parks which were once no-go areas are now safe to walk about by day.

" The New York populace can be divided into three groups, those virtuous, those shamed into obedience and those fearful only of corporal punishment. Police must guard the first from danger, prevent or dissuade the second from descending, and frustrate or punish the third. "

**Charles Christian,
Magistrate of Police, 1812**

Despite the statistics, there is still a nervous edge to the streets, a palpable sense of imminent danger. You are most unlikely to be mugged but it doesn't always feel like that. In part this is what makes New York so exciting – but it does mean that you need to keep your wits about you and to know when it is best to walk away.

Harlem and the Heights

There is downtown, midtown and uptown, and then there is the rest. Many maps of Manhattan stop at Central Park, but that is to ignore almost half of the island. The real uptown lies far to the north, beyond the skyscrapers and the shopping malls. This is where you find Harlem, described by Nelson Mandela as 'the capital of the black world'.

HARLEM AND THE HEIGHTS

Harlem and the Heights

Getting there: **Subway:** *A, B, C, D, 2, 3 to 125th St or 135th St for Harlem; B, C, 1, 9 to 110th St or 116th St for Morningside Heights; A for Washington Heights.* **Bus:** *M4 for The Cloisters and Washington Heights; M5 for Morningside Heights and scenic Riverside Drive.*

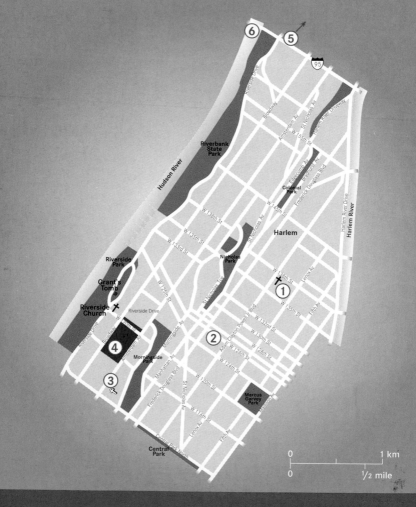

① *Abyssinian Baptist Church*

The biggest and best-known of Harlem's many black churches is famed for its charismatic gospel services. This is one of a number of Harlem churches which welcome visitors to share in their worship on Sundays. **Page 147**

② *Apollo Theater*

Ella Fitzgerald, Sarah Vaughan and Gladys Knight all launched their careers at the Apollo, and the Wednesday amateur nights are still the best place to see the jazz and hip-hop stars of the next generation. **Pages 147, 153**

③ *Cathedral of St. John the Divine*

If this building is ever finished it will be the largest cathedral in the world, big enough to hold both Notre Dame and Chartres under one roof. Until then it is better known as a centre of social activism and the home of the National AIDS Memorial.
Pages 148–149

④ *Columbia University*

This prestigious Ivy League university is at the heart of a lively student area of cafés, bookstores and bars. The steps outside the Low Library, overlooking the main quadrangle, are a popular summer hangout. **Page 149**

⑤ *The Cloisters*

An inspired piece of modern architecture or the ultimate Rockefeller folly? This outpost of the Metropolitan Museum consists of a group of European monasteries rebuilt on a bluff overlooking the Hudson River. **Pages 150–151**

⑥ *George Washington Bridge*

Cass Gilbert's bridge across the Hudson is all the more admired because the developers ran out of funds and had to leave the steel towers uncovered. Le Corbusier called it the most beautiful bridge in the world. **Page 151**

Harlem

'You must take the A train to go to Sugar Hill way up in Harlem. If you miss the A train you'll find you've missed the quickest way to Harlem.' *You can still take the A train to Harlem, with Duke Ellington's music ringing in your ears, but many people are simply too scared. There are numerous stories of careless tourists, meandering uptown on the subway, who realised with horror after 59th Street that they were on an express train to Harlem and that theirs was the only white face in the carriage. Many white visitors do feel out of place in Harlem – but although there are pockets of danger here as everywhere else, the frisson of fear that many people experience as they step off the train is largely misplaced.*

Founded by Dutch settlers and named New Haarlem because of its distance from New Amsterdam, Harlem was once a rural retreat for the wealthy of Lower Manhattan. It was only in the early 20th century that black people arriving from the South began moving into its handsome brownstone houses. Between 1900 and 1920 the black population of New York tripled and most of the new arrivals settled in Harlem. In those days, writes Eddy L Harris, Harlem 'had the power to make black people feel free just by being here'.

The Jazz Age of the 1920s was known as the Harlem Renaissance, when Cab Calloway played in the whites-only Cotton Club and Manhattan enjoyed 'the negro vogue'. As the writer Langston Hughes pointed out, the Renaissance was essentially a white creation which did little to raise the living standards of ordinary black people. When the Depression came in the 1930s, Harlem entered a spiral of decline; before long it had become a worldwide symbol of

urban decay, epitomised by the riots and burned-out buildings of the 1960s. Now, at last, there is talk of a second Harlem Renaissance, as upwardly-mobile black professionals return to their roots and businesses are attracted to the new Harlem USA shopping mall.

Harlem's brownstone houses are being restored and are once again fashionable places to live. Sugar Hill, where Count Basie and Duke Ellington had their homes, is part of the **Hamilton Heights Historic District** – named after the first Treasury Secretary, Alexander Hamilton, whose farmhouse is now a museum. Further south, **Mount Morris Park Historic District** on 122nd Street contains a monument to a remarkable Harlem woman, Mother Clara Hale, who took in hundreds of babies abandoned by drug-addicted mothers in the 1970s and 1980s. The monument has been funded by, among others, Rupert Murdoch, Yoko Ono and Donald Trump.

" *Harlem was the promised land, where black men and women came to escape, to reach beyond the grasp they would have been able to reach for in the places they came from … to dream the dreams that might have gone unimagined.* "

Eddy L Harris, *Still Life in Harlem*, **1996**

Many people visit Harlem on a 'gospel tour', with a church service included (*page 23*). This is fine, but to avoid the impression of voyeurism it is important to keep your camera away and to remember that you are in a place of worship. The **Abyssinian Baptist Church** (*132 W 138th St*) has one of the best gospel choirs; the former Congressman and civil rights leader Adam Clayton Powell Jr was minister here for many years. In Harlem, 7th Avenue becomes Adam Clayton Powell Boulevard; 6th Avenue is named after Malcolm X, who preached in the Malcolm Shabazz mosque (*16th St*).

The streets of Harlem resonate with the memories of 20th-century black Americans, from Louis Armstrong to Stevie Wonder and the Harlem Globetrotters. This is still the spiritual home of African–American culture. Visit Harlem on a Wednesday and you can catch Amateur Night at the **Apollo Theater** (*page 145*), the making of Ella Fitzgerald and nearly the unmaking of Diana Ross.

Getting there: Subway: A, B, C, C, D, 2, 3 to 125th St; B, C, 2, 3 to 135th St.

Morningside Heights

Washington defeated the British here at the Battle of Harlem Heights, but West Harlem remained a quiet rural backwater until the end of the 19th century, with the building of a new cathedral and university and the construction of Riverside Drive. In the 1960s, as Harlem acquired negative connotations, residents rechristened the area Morningside Heights.

Cathedral of St. John the Divine

Amsterdam Ave at W 112th St. Tel: 212–316–7540. Subway: 1, 9, B, C to Cathedral Parkway–110th St. Open: daily 0900–1700. Admission free.

When work began on this massive cathedral in 1892, it was designed to be built in the Romanesque style; by 1911 a new architect had changed the focus to French Gothic. The work was suspended during World War II and only resumed in 1978, with many people arguing that the money should be spent on social projects instead. If the church is ever completed it will be the largest cathedral in the world, 600 ft long with seating for 10,000 people. It will probably take another 50 years.

The cathedral has become known as a centre for radical Christianity, social action and avant-garde art. The **Peace Fountain** in the garden is surrounded by children's sculptures. A carving on the front portal shows the Manhattan skyline under a

mushroom cloud. Inside, look for the **Poetry Wall** – where nothing is ever rejected – and the AIDS chapel on the south side of the nave. The bookshop contains a model of the design for the finished cathedral, as well as books on Taoism and non-racist parenting.

This church has never shied away from controversy – in the 1970s it was at the forefront of the campaign for women priests. Annual events include a celebration of the winter solstice, a service for American Indians and a blessing of the animals on the first Sunday in October.

Columbia University

Broadway and 116th St. Tel: 212–854–1754. Subway: 1, 9 to 116th St–Columbia University.

> **"** New York, the city where one is only motionless on a psychiatrist's couch or a mortuary slab. **"**
>
> **Barry Pilton, *An Innocent Abroad*, 1997**

Founded as King's College in 1754, New York's most prestigious university moved to its present site in 1897. The buildings, designed in the Beaux Arts style by McKim, Mead and White, are laid out around a central grassy quadrangle. The most impressive is the **Low Library**, whose steps may be familiar as the setting for anti-Vietnam War demos in the 1960s. These days the steps are invariably crowded with students relaxing between classes.

Grant's Tomb

Riverside Drive at 122nd St. Tel: 212–666–1640. Subway: 1, 9 to 116th St–Columbia University. Bus: M5. Open: daily 0900–1700. Admission free.

The Civil War hero **Ulysses S Grant** (1822–85) later became President of the United States and he is buried alongside his wife in this Greek-style mausoleum, whose interior was inspired by Napoleon's tomb in Paris. Outside, in stunning contrast to the black marble tombs, are a set of Gaudiesque mosaic benches, designed by Chilean artist **Pedro Silva** and created by local schoolchildren in the 1970s.

Riverside Church

Riverside Drive at 122nd St. Tel: 212–870–6700. Subway: 1, 9 to 116th St–Columbia University. Bus: M5. Open: daily 0900–1600. Service: Sun 1045. Admission free.

This huge interdenominational church, financed by John D Rockefeller Jr, was built in the 1930s in 'skyscraper Gothic' style. The carillon here is the largest in the world, with 74 bells weighing up to 20 tons each. You can take the elevator to the 20th floor and climb to the bell tower for **panoramic views** of Upper Manhattan – though it's probably best to avoid going up when the bells are ringing.

Washington Heights

The far north of Manhattan is known as Little Santo Domingo on account of its large Dominican population. There is also a community of Chino-Latinos, Cantonese emigrants from Hong Kong who arrived in the United States via Cuba. This area, which was once rolling farmland, contains some of the oldest houses in Manhattan as well as its most surprising museum.

The Cloisters

Fort Tryon Park. Tel: 212–923–3700. Subway: A to 190th St. Bus: M4. Open: Mar–Oct, Tue–Sun 0930–1715 (Nov–Feb, 0930–1645). Admission: **.

It could only ever happen in New York. The sculptor George Barnard scoured the abandoned monasteries of France, picking

up pieces of medieval art from derelict cellars and barns; John D Rockefeller Jr (who else?) purchased the collection and gave it to the Metropolitan Museum; Rockefeller then bought Fort Tryon Park for the city and provided the funds for a modern museum incorporating five complete Romanesque and Gothic courtyards. He even bought the Palisades, across the river in New Jersey, to ensure that the views from The Cloisters would remain unspoilt.

This is a remarkable and special place, combining fragmented elements from different regions and centuries into a unified whole. The buildings, including a 12th-century chapel from Spain and a chapter house from a French abbey, act as a treasury for a fine collection of religious painting, sculpture and stained glass. One highlight is the **Unicorn Tapestries**, a set of six late medieval tapestries depicting the unicorn legend, woven in Brussels around 1500 and discovered in a French barn in 1850 after being used to protect fruit trees from frost.

The cloisters themselves fulfil their original purpose of providing a peaceful setting in which to contemplate your surroundings. One of them, the **Bonnefont Cloister**, contains a medieval herb garden overlooking the Hudson. Afterwards you can take a walk through **Fort Tryon Park**, a strip of wooded parkland criss-crossed by winding paths.

George Washington Bridge

Subway: A to 175th St; 1, 9 to 181st St. Bus: M4, M5.

> **"** The west side of the island was rich in façades not unlike the possibilities of a fairy princess with syphilis. **"**
>
> **Richard Condon**

A bridge linking Manhattan to New Jersey was more than 60 years in the planning, and even when it opened in 1931 it was still not complete. The original plans involved sheathing the towers in granite, but when the money ran out they were left as the skeletal steel structures that New Yorkers have grown to love. The Swiss architect **Le Corbusier**, who called New York 'a beautiful catastrophe', said of the Washington Bridge that this was where 'steel architecture seems to laugh'. To see what he meant, walk across the bridge with the tugboats far beneath you, or see it at night from Riverside Park. On the Circle Line cruise around Manhattan (*page 43*), you get a close-up view of the lighthouse featured in Hildegarde Swift's children's book *The Little Red Lighthouse and the Great Gray Bridge*. The lighthouse was saved from demolition in the 1950s after children wrote letters on its behalf.

Morris-Jumel Mansion

*65 Jumel Terrace at 160th St. Tel: 212–923–8008. Subway: B, C to 163rd St. Open: Wed–Sun 1000–1600. Admission: *.*

Manhattan's oldest house was built by Lt Col Roger Morris in 1765 and briefly used by George Washington as his base. It was later bought by Stephen Jumel, a wine merchant from France who furnished it in Napoleonic style. After his death, his wife Eliza, a former prostitute, scandalised New York society by marrying the elderly former Vice-President Aaron Burr and divorcing him on the day of his death. The clapboard house has been refurbished in period style, with some of the Jumels' original furniture.

Restaurants and clubs

The days when Harlem had a jazz club on every corner are long gone, but there are still several places where you can combine a little soul food with some live entertainment.

Copeland's
547 W 145th St. Tel: 212–234–2357.
**. The Southern dishes here range from braised oxtail to Louisiana gumbo. There is live jazz on Friday and Saturday nights and an uplifting Sunday gospel brunch.

Jimmy's Uptown
2207 Seventh Ave (between 130th and 131st St). Tel: 212–491–4000. **.
A spacious, trendy club that highlights Harlem's historic renaissance.

Miss Maude's
547 Lenox Ave (between 137th and 138th Sts). Tel: 212–690–3100. *.
An easy-going Harlem eatery, you can eat vast quantities of excellent food at low prices.

Sugar Hill Bistro
458 W 145th St (between Amsterdam and Convent Aves). Tel: 212–491–5505. ***.
Near the beautiful brownstones of Harlem's highest hill, Sugar Hill Bistro is spread over four floors. Come here for good, eclectic Southern cuisine, live jazz on weekends and gospel singers at Sunday brunch.

Londel's
2620 Frederick Douglass Blvd between 139th and 140th Sts. Tel: 212–234–6114. **. This trendy Sugar Hill supper club, run by a former policeman, is where Harlem's 'buppies' come to dine on nouvelle soul classics like snapper in lobster sauce. You might catch some jazz here on Friday and Saturday nights.

Amy Ruth's
113 W 116th St (between Lenox and Seventh Aves). Tel: 212–280–8779. *.
Come here for the best Southern food north of the Mason–Dixon line. You'll get huge portions of great eats served at bargain prices.

Sylvia's
328 Lenox Ave (between 126th and 127th Sts). Tel: 212–996–0660. **.
The 'Queen of Soul Food' has been turning out fried chicken and beef ribs since 1962. Come here for giant portions of old-style Southern cuisine, and remember to leave some room for the sweet potato pie. Get here early for the Sunday gospel brunch.

Bayou
308 Lenox Ave (between 125th and 126th Sts.). Tel: 212–426–3800. **.
An excellent place for Cajun–Creole and some New Orleans kinds of food.

Charles' Southern-Style Kitchen
2839 Eighth Ave (between 151st and 152nd Sts). Tel: 212–926–4313. *.
Eat like a king at this no-frills Harlem heaven. The buffet of crisp, juicy, fried chicken and other treats are excellent.

Shopping

*Harlem's main shopping drag, 125th Street, has a number of stores selling cut-price clothes as well as CDs of reggae and rap music. **Mart 125**, facing the Apollo, is an indoor street market specialising in African clothing and crafts. As part of the regeneration of Harlem, this area is currently undergoing redevelopment and by the year 2000 it will be home to a new **Harlem USA** theme mall. The market traders who used to work on 125th Street have been moved to the **Malcolm Shabazz market** on the corner of 116th Street and Malcolm X Boulevard.*

Music

Apollo Theater

253 W 125th St. Tel: 212–222–0992.

All the great names of black American music have appeared at the Apollo, the only survivor of more than 30 vaudeville theatres in Harlem. Ella Fitzgerald and Michael Jackson launched their careers by winning its Wednesday Amateur Night talent show; Diana Ross and Luther Vandross were booed off the stage. The audiences are still just as ruthless and anyone who can survive Amateur Night has probably got a showbiz future ahead of them. These days the Amateur Nights are shown on TV and they remain one of the best nights out in Manhattan. Look out for gigs featuring hip-hop, rap, jazz and blues.

Soul food

Soul food is the cuisine of the American Deep South. This is hearty home cooking, rooted in the land and the experiences of African and Caribbean slaves. Typical soul food dishes include fried chicken, barbecued ribs, black-eyed peas, corn muffins, collard greens (boiled spiced cabbage), candied yams and grits (boiled crushed maize).

Harlem

In the eighteenth century, Harlem emerged as a Manhattan getaway for wealthy downtowners. They gave way to a succession of immigrants – Jews, Irish and then, in the early 1900s, Blacks, who turned it into the capital of Black America. Harlem saw its heyday in the 1920s and '30s, when artists including Ella Fitzgerald and Duke Ellington played at venues such the Savoy and Cotton Club, long since gone.

One of the early cultural centres in Harlem was the Harlem YMCA, where Langston Hughes gave poetry reading sessions. 125th Street bustled with the energy and excitement of any main street. But with the flight of a growing middle class and an influx of drugs and crime, Harlem slid into a decay from which it is only now emerging. More people are moving into the elegant brownstones and new housing, and the neighbourhood is an attractive and popular place for tourists.

Restaurants such as Jimmy's Uptown and Amy Ruth's are attracting large crowds of people; together with the legendary Charles' Southern-Style Kitchen, they offer what many consider the best soul food in the city. The Lenox Lounge was recently renovated and has regular jazz sessions. The most popular destination remains 125th Street, the thriving main strip in Harlem.

The 86-year-old **Apollo Theater** is where Aretha Franklin, Billie Holiday and Count Bassie performed. The **Schomburg Center for Research on Black Culture**, the **Studio Museum** and the **National Black Theater** (*tel: 212–722– 3800*) have strong roots in Harlem and their frequent exhibitions testify to the importance of Black culture.

Studio Museum in Harlem

144 W 125th St (between Lenox Ave and Adam Clayton Powell Blvd). Tel: 212–864–4500. www.studiomuseumharlemharlem.org. Subway: 2, 3 to 125th St. Open: Wed–Fri 1000–1700, Sat–Sun 1300–1800, Tue: group tours (call in advance).

Dedicated to African–American art, as well as to work from Africa and the Diaspora, this museum for artists was built in 1967. The museum organises thematic and single artist exhibitions, and its permanent collection includes work by Romare Bearden, Jacob Lawrence and Norman Lewis. The building also houses studios, workshops and a museum shop.

Schomburg Center for Research on Black Culture

515 Malcolm X Blvd (at 135th St). Tel: 212–491–2200.
The Schomburg Center is built around the personal collection of Arturo Alfonso Schomburg, a Puerto Rican bibliophile and scholar of Black culture, who died in Brooklyn in 1938. His personal collection was added to the Division of Negro Literature, History and Prints of the 135th Street branch of the New York Public Library in 1926. It has grown to include more than five million items – books, manuscripts, art, audio, video and even sheets of music – documenting the history and culture of people of African descent throughout the world.

The Project

427 W 126th St (between Morningside and Amsterdam Aves). Tel: 212–662– 8610.
The writer Christian Haye started this interesting new development in the Harlem contemporary art scene in 1999. The project has brought an international list of young artists from Europe, Asia, Africa and the United States to a cosmopolitan section of Manhattan. Recent exhibits have shown the works of Paul Pfeiffer, Tom Gidley and Martin Weber.

Hamilton Grange National Memorial

287 Convent Ave (between 141st and 142nd Sts). Tel: 212–283–5154.
A quaint country house built in 1802 that was once the country home of Alexander Hamilton – the first US Secretary of the Treasury. Hamilton lived in Hamilton Grange with his family for only two years before he was killed in a duel with Aaron Burr in 1804. Given landmark status many years ago, the Grange now stands amid busy streets near the City College campus.

Brooklyn and the Outer Boroughs

To many people, New York simply means Manhattan – but spend a day in Brooklyn, or any of the outer boroughs, and you discover a very different city, of tree-lined streets and historic neighbourhoods where the views stretch further than the nearest skyscraper. Outside Manhattan, there is more room to breathe and the air is just that little bit more relaxed.

Brooklyn and the Outer Boroughs

*Getting there: **Subway:** 2, 3 to Eastern Parkway–Brooklyn Museum, or walk across Brooklyn Bridge. The main sights in Brooklyn are linked by a trolley-bus service that operates on summer weekends.*

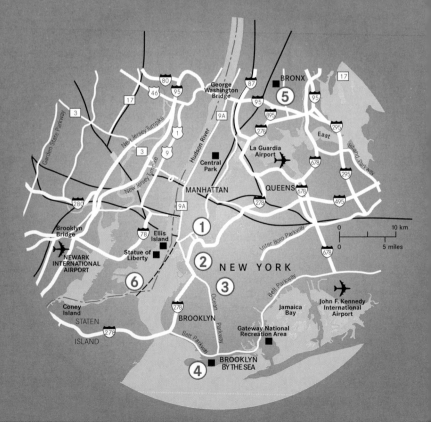

① *Brooklyn Bridge*

When this bridge opened in 1883, linking Brooklyn with Manhattan for the first time, it was the longest suspension bridge in the world. There is still no better way to approach Manhattan than to walk across Brooklyn Bridge at dusk. **Page 162**

② *Brooklyn Heights Promenade*

To get the best views of Lower Manhattan you need to cross into Brooklyn and stroll along this handsome esplanade. The Federal-style row houses of Brooklyn Heights are some of the most expensive in New York. **Page 163**

③ *Brooklyn Museum of Art*

The original plans were to build the world's largest museum, and although these have not succeeded it does contain world-class collections of Egyptian and African art as well as American painting and architecture. **Pages 164–165**

④ *Coney Island*

In the 1920s this was known as 'Poor Man's Paradise', where anyone could have an afternoon on the beach for the price of a subway token. The rusting fairground rides are still in operation but they have now been designated historic landmarks. **Page 165**

⑤ *Bronx Zoo*

The largest urban zoo in the United States keeps its animals in simulated natural habitats, from the Himalayan highlands to the African plains. There is even a World of Darkness, where nocturnal species are kept awake by day. **Page 166**

⑥ *Staten Island Ferry*

The ride which has inspired movies and songs is still one of the most romantic experiences in New York. It is even better at night, with Manhattan twinkling in the distance. Best of all, it's free. **Page 167**

Brooklyn

The word is out – Brooklyn is hot. Artists are setting up studios on the waterfront in Williamsburg and Red Hook. The derelict Navy Yard is being turned into the world's biggest film studio. Cutting-edge theatre and dance companies are arriving from Manhattan, and America's oldest opera house has become a showcase for the avant-garde. Even tourists are coming to Brooklyn – the first luxury hotel for 70 years opened in 1998 and the borough is now included on open-top bus tours.

If Brooklyn were anywhere but New York, it would get a lot more attention. This was, after all, the third city in America when it was annexed in 1898 and with a population of 2.3 million it would still be one of the largest. More people live in Brooklyn than in any other New York borough. It has more black people than Harlem, more Jews than the Lower East Side, more Italians than Little Italy. It has a world-class museum, a beautiful park and a fine sandy beach. Its biggest problem is that it is too close to Manhattan.

Founded as Breukelen by early Dutch settlers, Brooklyn remained a quiet rural retreat on the tip of Long Island until the opening of a steamboat service to Manhattan in 1814 brought it within easy reach of commuters. An advertisement of the time, from landowner Hezekiah Pierpont, said that 'gentlemen whose business or profession require their daily attendance in the city cannot better, or with less expense, secure the health and comfort of their families than by moving to Brooklyn Heights'. **Federal and Greek Revival brownstone houses** were built close to the ferry landing, and they remain some of New York's most desirable addresses today. The difference now is that they are also some of the most expensive.

This is New York's most racially diverse borough, from Little Poland in Greenpoint to an emigré Russian community on **Brighton Beach**. **Crown Heights** and **Bedford-Stuyvesant** have large African–American populations, who arrived in the 1930s on the 'A' train from Harlem. Neighbouring **Fort Greene**, with its funky bistros and cafés, has recently been dubbed 'the black East Village'. **Williamsburg** is home to Puerto Ricans and Hassidic Jews, and **Atlantic Avenue** in Brooklyn Heights to a large Middle Eastern community.

One in seven Americans can trace their roots to Brooklyn. **Woody Allen** claims to have grown up beneath the Cyclone roller coaster on Coney Island. **Neil Simon** grew up in Brighton Beach. Brooklyn has produced **George Gershwin**, **Al Capone**, **Mel Brooks**, **Barbra Streisand**, **Spike Lee** and **Rudolph Giuliani**. It also produced the famous Brooklyn accent, where 'this' becomes 'dis' and 'first' becomes 'foist'. As gentrification spreads and the accent disappears, it is being recorded for posterity by the Long Island Historical Society.

Brooklyn is more spread out than Manhattan, but most of the main sights are within a short distance of one another. For a day out from Manhattan, take the subway to the museum and spend an hour or two exploring its collections; walk through the Botanic Garden to Prospect Park; return to Brooklyn Heights on the subway and stroll along the Promenade before crossing back over Brooklyn Bridge at sunset. On summer weekends a free tram service connects the museum and Botanic Garden with Prospect Park and the children's zoo.

Brooklyn Bridge

Subway: 4, 5, 6 to Brooklyn Bridge–City Hall; A, C to High St–Brooklyn Bridge.

'All that trouble just to get to Brooklyn'. This was the joke going around in 1883, but the real purpose of the bridge was to bring Brooklyn to New York. In many ways this magnificent structure can be seen as the origin of the modern city. Physically, because it provided the link which paved the way for the creation of Greater New York. Aesthetically, because in its blending of art and industry it anticipated the age of the skyscraper.

It was designed by John Roebling, a German engineer who died of gangrene before construction had even begun; his son, Washington Roebling, took over but he succumbed to an attack of 'the bends' while working in an underwater chamber and had to supervise the work from his sickbed in Brooklyn Heights. When it opened, this was the world's longest suspension bridge, the first to be made of steel and the second highest structure in New York. More than 150,000 people crossed the bridge on its opening day. A week later, 12 people were crushed to death in the mass panic that followed when a woman tripped and fell.

John Travolta may have danced on the railings in *Saturday Night Fever*, but most people will be content to walk, listening to the rumble of the traffic as the walkway trembles beneath your feet. Crossing from Brooklyn, Manhattan appears through a Gothic portal, the symbolic entrance to the city – and the skyscrapers of the Financial District loom up through a spider's web of suspension cables that have been likened to a giant harp.

Brooklyn Heights

Subway: M, N, R to Court St; 2, 3 to Clark St; 2, 3, 4, 5 to Borough Hall.

'I live in Brooklyn. By choice.' So wrote Truman Capote, author of *Breakfast at Tiffany's*, written in a house on Brooklyn Heights. Living in the Heights, he added, 'secures a seagull's view of the Manhattan and Brooklyn bridges, of lower Manhattan's tall dazzle and the ship-lane waters, breeding river to bay to ocean, that encircle and seethe past posturing Miss Liberty'.

With its 19th-century row houses and tree-lined streets, Brooklyn Heights is one of the most appealing neighbourhoods of the city. This was the first area in New York to be declared a historic district under the landmarks legislation of 1965. The main attraction is the **Promenade**, the most romantic spot in New York for a first date. When you tire of the Manhattan skyline, come here and see it again through new eyes. Beneath you to your right, the old Fulton ferry district has become a hip waterfront neighbourhood of restaurants and art galleries which goes by the acronym DUMBO (Down Under Manhattan Bridge Overpass).

There are more chic restaurants and bars on Montague Street, the laid-back main drag, which leads from the Promenade to **Borough Hall**, a Greek Revival pile built in 1848 to rival City Hall in Manhattan. Near here you can find the shops and restaurants of **Atlantic Avenue** (*page 169*). Back on Montague Street, look out for the church of **St. Ann and the Holy Trinity**, which contains some of America's earliest stained glass. The church is now used as a venue for concerts, with an emphasis on the avant-garde.

> **"** *You date in Manhattan, marry in Long Island and breed in Brooklyn.* **"**
>
> **Jim Keeble,** *Sunday Telegraph***, 1998**

Brooklyn Museum of Art

200 Eastern Parkway. Tel: 718–638–5000. www.brooklynart.org.
Subway: 2, 3 to Eastern Parkway–Brooklyn Museum. Open: Wed–Fri
*1000–1700, Sat 1100–2100, Sun 1100–1800. Admission: *.*

This was supposed to be the world's largest museum but it is not even the biggest in New York. In the late 19th century, when Brooklyn had ambitions to overtake Manhattan, the city asked Charles McKim to design a Beaux Arts temple of learning; by the time it was completed, Brooklyn was a mere borough and the museum was a sixth of its originally planned size.

While the Met was collecting Old Masters, the Brooklyn Museum concentrated on African and American art. The American paintings include Gilbert Stuart's portrait of George Washington and Georgia O'Keeffe's *Brooklyn Bridge*, as well as 19th-century paintings by Albert Bierstadt, Edward Hicks and John Singer Sargent. A series of American period rooms begins with a 17th-century Dutch farmhouse in Brooklyn and includes John D Rockefeller's Moorish Smoking Room.

This was the first museum in America to display African objects as art; the outstanding collection includes ceremonial masks and a carved ivory gong from Benin. The Ancient Egyptian collection, with decorated mummy cases and a gilded ibis coffin, is also among the finest in the world. Other highlights are Native American totem poles; textiles from Peru; 19th-century French painting; and a collection of Rodin sculptures. The Sculpture Garden contains fragments of demolished New York buildings including Pennsylvania Station, tenement houses and a Coney Island lamp-post.

This museum is a lot less crowded than the Met and you can explore the highlights in a couple of hours. Afterwards, walk through the neighbouring **Brooklyn Botanic Garden** to reach **Prospect Park**. Designed by Olmsted and Vaux, the architects of Central Park, they considered Prospect Park their supreme achievement. When Mae West grew up in Brooklyn, 'gentlemen and deer ran wild in Prospect Park'; these days it is a shady outdoor playground, with a carousel, skating rink, boating lake and children's zoo, and concerts in the bandshell on summer weekends.

Brooklyn-by-the-Sea

Subway: B, D, F, N to Coney Island; D, Q to Brighton Beach or Sheepshead Bay. The funfairs are open daily from June to August and weekends from April to October.

Djuna Barnes visited **Coney Island** in 1914 and described a working-class summer playground of dance halls and gambling dens, funfairs and carousels, freak shows on the boardwalk and a game which involved throwing baseballs at a ducking negro. This was where Nathan Handwerker invented the hot dog and where Cary Grant began his career as a 'man on stilts'. Coney Island, where the Atlantic surf washes the New York shore, was Brooklyn-by-the-Sea.

The sideshows and the clam stalls are still there, but get here soon – a sports stadium and theme mall are being built and gentrification cannot be far behind. **The Cyclone**, the world's first wooden roller coaster in 1927, still operates; Charles Lindbergh said it was more thrilling than flying the Atlantic. Another landmark is the **Wonder Wheel**, built in 1920 by the Eccentric Ferris Wheel Company and offering distant views of Manhattan. The Parachute Jump, built in 1939 for the World's Fair, still stands but is no longer in use.

A wooden boardwalk leads past **New York Aquarium** to **Brighton Beach**, named after Brighton in England and developed as a fashionable resort in the 1870s. Fred Astaire and the Marx Brothers used to play in the theatres here, but these days it is better known for its Russian nightclubs (*page 169*). More than 30,000 Russians have arrived in Brighton Beach since 1970, and the shops of 'Little Odessa' sell caviar and rye bread. West of Brighton Beach, **Sheepshead Bay** has a laid-back fishing village atmosphere, with boats offering deep-sea fishing expeditions and restaurants on the harbour which will cook your catch while you wait.

" *In a town of immigrants, you twitch a string in Brooklyn, someone dies in Moscow.* "

Reggie Nadelson, Independent, 1995

The other boroughs

Although Brooklyn is the easiest and most rewarding of the outer boroughs to explore, each of the others can make for an enjoyable day out from Manhattan.

The Bronx

Named after a Swedish sailor, Jonas Bronck, who bought a farm here in the 17th century, the Bronx is the only one of New York's boroughs to be attached to the American mainland. To many people the name conjures up images of poverty, violence and urban despair, but there is more to the Bronx than that and even the notorious South Bronx is less threatening than it was. Two sights worth visiting are the **New York Botanical Garden** *tel: 718–817–8700 (subway: D, 4 to Bedford Park Blvd; *)* and **Bronx Zoo**, now known as the International Wildlife Conservation Park, *Subway: 2, 5 to E Tremont Ave; **; free on Wed)*, where 4000 animals live in re-creations of their natural habitats. You can see some of them from a monorail or from the Skyfari cable car. In the South Bronx, **Yankee Stadium** *(subway: B, D, 4 to 161st St)* is the home of the New York Yankees, winners of the World Series baseball in 1998. Matches take place between April and October; you can also take a tour of the ground where Babe Ruth and Joe Di Maggio made their names *(tel: 718–579–4531 for details)*.

Queens

The most sprawling and suburban of New York's five boroughs has a population of more than two million, but most visitors only see it on the taxi ride from JFK to Manhattan. In the late 20th century, Queens became the borough of choice for new immigrants to New York. **Flushing** is New York's second Chinatown, and also home to **Flushing Meadow-Corona Park** *(subway: 7 to Willets Point–Shea Stadium)*, the venue for the US Open Tennis championship. The park contains the New York Mets baseball stadium, an interactive science museum and a hollow steel Unisphere built for the 1964 World's Fair. **Astoria** is Little Athens, the largest Greek community in

America and at one time the centre of the world film industry. **The American Museum of the Moving Image**, in the old Paramount studios, features movie memorabilia, special effects and screenings of old films (*35th Ave at 36th St. Tel: 718–392–5600. Subway: G, R to Steinway St; N to Broadway. Open: Tue–Fri 1200–1700, Sat–Sun 1100–1800. Admission: ****).

Staten Island

Subway: 1, 9 to South Ferry, then ferry to Staten Island.

Staten Island does not really belong in New York at all. This was the message of its voters in a non-binding 1993 referendum that voted for secession from New York City. The borough, which constantly votes Republican in an overwhelmingly Democratic city, was fed up with being treated as Manhattan's garbage dump (Staten Island contains the world's largest landfill site) and decided it would like to keep its precious green landscape to itself.

Everyone goes to Staten Island once just to take the **Staten Island ferry**, sailing through New York harbour with Manhattan receding into the distance. The ferry, launched in 1905, runs day and night and the service is completely free. This has to be one of the world's most romantic boat rides. Most people turn straight round at Staten Island and head back to Manhattan, but if you want to explore further, take the S74 bus to **Historic Richmondtown** *Tel: 718–351–1611* (*open: Wed–Sun 1300–1700; weekends only in winter; **), an outdoor museum of 17th- to 19th-century buildings in the island's former capital, and the **Jacques Marchais Museum of Tibetan Art** *Tel: 718–987–3500* (*open: Apr–Oct, Wed–Sun 1300–1700; **), housed in a Buddhist-style hilltop temple.

> **"** *New York impressed me tremendously because, more than any other city in the world, it is the fullest expression of our modern age.* **"**
>
> **Leon Trotsky (1879–1940), former resident of the Bronx**

Restaurants in Brooklyn

Loulou
*222 Dekalb Avenue (between Adelphi and Claremont Ave). Tel: 212–246–0633. **.* This popular and very cosy restaurant boasts of authentic Gallic coastal cuisine and delightful service.

Monte's Italian
*451 Carroll St. (between Nevins St and 3rd Ave). Tel: 718–624–8984. **.* A traditional Italian restaurant, founded in 1918, that provides great sauces that you can't refuse.

Brawta
*347 Atlantic Ave (Hoyt St). Tel: 718–855–5515. **.* Jamaican classics like jerk chicken as well as blue snapper stew and home-made ginger beer in an open-plan kitchen with Caribbean art on the walls. Bring your own beer.

New City Bar and Grill
*25 Lafayette Ave (between Ashland Pl and Felix St). Tel: 718–875–7197. **.* A good place to stop by when visiting the Brooklyn Art Museum. A delicious New American menu.

Cucina
*256 5th Ave, Park Slope. Tel: 718–230–0711. ***.* Many people rate this Tuscan pasta joint the best restaurant in Brooklyn. Come here for lunch then walk it off with a stroll through Prospect Park.

Gage & Tollner
*372 Fulton St (Jay St). Tel: 718–875–5181. ***.* This 1879 steak-and-seafood landmark has been recently restored with mahogany-framed mirrors and the original gaslights. Mae West and Muhammad Ali are among the previous clients here.

The Grocery
*288 Smith St (between Sackett and Union Sts). Tel: 718–596–3335. **.* One of Carroll Garden's creative places with excellent, ambitious New American fare with an oriental slant. The warm welcome and hip *haute cuisine* keep its devotees happy.

Grimaldi's
*19 Old Fulton St. Tel: 718–858–4300. *.* You may have to wait in line for a pizza but it is the best pizza in New York, cooked in a brick oven and piled high with mozzarella and Italian tomatoes.

Junior's
*386 Flatbush Ave (Dekalb Ave). Tel: 718–852–5257. *.* This bustling downtown diner is known for its oversized sandwiches and gut-busting cheesecakes.

Garden Café
*620 Vanderbilt Ave (Prospect Pl). Tel: 718–857–8863. **.* A quiet Prospect Heights find – come here for spectacular New American food.

Areo
*8424 3rd Ave (85th St). Tel: 718–238–0079. **.* A perpetually crowded Bay Ridge Italian restaurant, offering fabulous food in big portions.

Relish
*225 Wythe Ave (between Metropolitan Ave and 3rd St). Tel: 718–96–4546. **.* Williamsburg diner fans love this picturesque place for its comfort food, moderate prices and unpretentious air.

Old Mexico
115 Montague St. Tel: 718–624–9774.
**. This wood-panelled restaurant in
the basement of a Brooklyn Heights
brownstone serves authentic Spanish
and Mexican (not Tex-Mex) cuisine.

Pete's Downtown
2 Water St. Tel: 718–858–3510. **.
Italian–American cooking and great
views of Manhattan from a waterfront
restaurant nestling beneath the
Brooklyn Bridge.

Peter Luger Steakhouse
*178 Broadway, Williamsburg.
Tel: 718–387–7400.* ***.
Williamsburg may seem an unlikely
venue for the best steaks in New York,
but nobody seriously disputes that
they are the best. There is really only
one thing to order here – porterhouse
steak, aged on the premises and grilled
to perfection, pink in the middle and
charred on the outside.

River Café
1 Water St. Tel: 718–522–5200.
***. Ask for a window table at this
celebrated New American restaurant,
which offers sublime seafood and
magical views of Manhattan from a
barge beneath the Brooklyn Bridge.
Men are required to wear a jacket
and jeans are not allowed.

Atlantic Avenue

The mile-long stretch of Atlantic Avenue, which begins in Brooklyn Heights,
has the flavour of a Middle Eastern souk, with Yemeni, Moroccan and
Lebanese restaurants and groceries like the **Sahadi Importing Company**
(187 Atlantic Ave), where sacks of chickpeas, flour and spices are piled
high on the floor.

This area has expanded beyond its Middle Eastern base to become a
thriving, multi-ethnic restaurant district. Besides those listed above, try **La
Bouillabaisse** (145 Atlantic Ave; tel: 718–522–8275) and **Petite Crevette**
(127 Atlantic Ave; tel: 718–858–6660) for seafood, **Caravan** (193 Atlantic
Ave; tel: 718–488–7111) for jazz and Moroccan cuisine, and **Moustache**
(405 Atlantic Ave; tel: 718–852–5555) for Jordanian 'pitzas'.

Moscow-by-the-Sea

The influx of Russians to Brighton Beach has prompted a rash of decadent
Russian nightclubs, where the vodka flows freely, the zakuski go on and
on and the floor shows feature acrobats, sequinned dancers and Sixties
disco hits. Go late, get on to the dance floor and try not to worry about
the Mafia lookalikes on the door – this is an unforgettable night out. The
best-known club is **Rasputin** (2670 Coney Island Ave; tel: 718–332–8111);
others are **Primorski** (282 Brighton Beach Ave; tel: 718–891–3111) and
National (273 Brighton Beach Ave; tel: 718–646–1225).

Peace and quiet in New York

One of the greatest myths about New York is that there is nowhere to relax – at least, nowhere apart from Central Park. In fact, even on Manhattan, there are plenty of places to escape the hustle of the city; try Battery Park (page 28), Riverside Park (page 137) and Fort Tryon Park (page 150). If you really want to get away from it all, though, you have to head for the outer boroughs.

Jamaica Bay

Tel: 718–318–4340. Subway: A to Broad Channel for Jamaica Bay Wildlife Refuge; S shuttle to Rockaway Beach.

This federal nature reserve between Brooklyn and Queens attracts 300 species of birds to a group of marshy islands the size of Manhattan. Herons and egrets breed here, and migrating wildfowl pass through in spring and autumn. There are footpaths and bird-watching hides, and guided ranger activities. **Rockaway Beach**, near by, has ten miles of boardwalk and sandy beach that is New York's top surfing spot in summer. This can get very crowded, but for more seclusion take the bus to the smaller beach at **Jacob Riis Park**, popular with gay men and naturists.

Staten Island Greenbelt

Tel: 718–667–2165. Bus: S74 to Rockland Ave from Staten Island ferry terminal at St. George.

At the centre of Staten Island, this 2500-acre reserve contains wetland, woodland and parkland habitats and 28 miles of hiking trails. Guided nature walks and other organised activities take place every weekend in summer. This is one of New York's best-kept secrets, just ten miles from downtown Manhattan.

Woodlawn Cemetery

Jerome and Bainbridge Aves. Tel: 718–920–0500. Subway: 4 to Woodlawn for Woodlawn Cemetery; 1, 9 to 242nd St for Van Cortlandt Park. Open: 0900–1600.

Manhattan ran out of burial space long ago, so the city's cemeteries are all located in the outer boroughs. This peaceful parkland cemetery in the North Bronx contains the graves of Duke Ellington and Miles Davis as well as the store owners Roland Macy and F W Woolworth – who is interred in a lavish pseudo-Egyptian mausoleum. You can pick up a guide at the cemetery entrance. Woodlawn Cemetery adjoins **Van Cortlandt Park**, which is bigger than Central Park and contains the Bronx's oldest house, the Georgian Colonial **Van Cortlandt Mansion**.

> " *New York is a great city to live in if you can afford to get out of it.* "
> **William Rossa Cole, 1992**

BROOKLYN AND THE OUTER BOROUGHS

Lifestyles

Shopping, eating, children and nightlife in New York

Shopping

New York is the shopping capital of the world. Many people fly here from Europe just to do their Christmas shopping or pick up some bargains in the January sales. From world-famous department stores to small, quirky shops selling nothing but buttons or human bones, New York has it all.

It is precisely because there is so much choice that many people get confused. You need to approach shopping in Manhattan with a clear head. There are lots of **good deals** around but it is easy to get carried away. Just because something costs less than it would at home does not mean you could not get it cheaper elsewhere. If you are serious about shopping, arrive with a list of target purchases, know what they cost at home and look in at least two or three stores before committing yourself. On the other hand, if you see a genuine bargain, snap it up. Shopping is a game in New York and taking a gamble is all part of the fun. In any case, there is nothing more frustrating than finding your way back to that discount store in Chelsea only to find that somebody else has just beaten you to that half-price fur coat you saw yesterday.

The lowdown

Most shops are open from around 1000–1800 Monday to Saturday, though many are **open late** on Thursdays and some department

stores stay open till 2000 every night. The majority of shops now open on Sundays, at least from 1200–1700. Bookstores, especially Barnes & Noble, and the Virgin Megastore on Times Square, are open late into the night.

The **price on the label** does not include sales tax, which is added at 8.25 per cent. This is not refundable, even for overseas visitors. If buying expensive items like jewellery, remember to allow for the customs duty which you may have to pay when you take it home.

Visitors from Europe need to remember that American **sizes** are different. As a rule of thumb, take one away from American shoe sizes to arrive at their British equivalents, and add two to the size of women's dresses.

Where to shop

Start at Saks **Fifth Avenue**, work your way up to **57th Street**, head one block east then turn uptown along **Madison** and you will have covered New York's most upmarket shopping district, home to the smartest department stores and the fashion houses' flagships. Other areas to consider are the **East Village** for funky clothes and vintage fashions; the **Lower East Side** and the **Garment District** for discount fashions; and **SoHo**, **Greenwich Village** and the **Upper West Side** for quirky, specialist shops (*see area chapters for listings*).

Malls

If you like your shopping experience predictable and you don't mind paying 'full retail', the various shopping malls offer a range of well-known names. The most fun is probably Pier 17 at **South Street Seaport**; others are at **Citicorp Center**, **Rockefeller Center**. Two malls which symbolise aspects of modern New York are **Trump Tower** (*5th Ave and 57th St*), a shrine to 1980s excess, and **Harlem USA** (*125th St*) a visible sign of Harlem's regeneration.

Department stores

Although they lack the cutting-edge excitement of some of the designer boutiques, Manhattan's department stores should be your first port of call if you are looking for clothes. **Macy's** and **Bloomingdales** are the biggest and best known, but for up-to-the-minute fashion you might do better in Barney's, Bergdorf Goodman or Henri Blendel. Shanghai Tang and Takashimaya are recent imports from China and Japan which are, conversely, both very New York. Saks Fifth Avenue is a solid department store which combines quality with style. All of these stores offer free personal shopping services – tell them what you are looking for and they will make a selection for you, and sometimes even deliver it to your hotel. You don't pay for the service but you are not exactly steered towards discounts – remember that the job of these people is to sell clothes.

Flea markets, street fairs and antique shops

At weekends the streets of Manhattan turn into open-air bazaars as households turn out their junk at neighbourhood street fairs. Stumble across one of these and you just might pick up a real bargain. This is less likely at the regular flea markets, but these are still great fun if you enjoy sifting through old records, Americana and piles of second-hand clothes. Two of the best, which take place every Saturday and Sunday, are at Broadway and Grand St in SoHo, and 6th Avenue from 24th to 27th Streets in Chelsea. For listings of other flea markets and street fairs, look in Friday's *New York Times*.

Antique shops are found in **Chelsea**, the **East Village** and along a short stretch of **Atlantic Avenue** in Brooklyn between Hoyt and Bond Streets. The Manhattan Art & Antiques Center (*2nd Ave at 55th St*) has more than a hundred galleries spread over three floors, offering furniture, silver, porcelain and Oriental art.

Museum shops

If you prefer museums to shopping, the museum gift shops are some of the classiest in New York. All offer a good selection of books and arts as well as stylish and unusual gifts. **The Museum of Modern Art** has its own design store, featuring the best of modern American design – a theme also taken up at the **Cooper-Hewitt Museum**. For books about New York, try the **Museum of the City of New York**; for kids' presents, the **Children's Museum of Manhattan** or the artSmart children's shop at the **Brooklyn Museum of Art**. As for the **Met**, it is difficult to escape shopping; there are not only shops scattered about the museum, but also in Macy's, the Rockefeller Center and SoHo.

What to buy

CDs:

These are much cheaper in the USA than elsewhere. The best selections are in the Virgin Megastore in **Times Square** and branches of Tower Records all over Manhattan.

Clothes:

At the top end of the scale, New York is home to the world's leading fashion houses, spread out along **Fifth** and **Madison Avenues**. Next come the chains, offering reliable, upmarket fashions – you will find branches of Ann Taylor, Banana Republic, Benetton, Gap, J. Crew, Limited and Express all over the city. Adventurous shoppers should head for the **discount stores**, offering designer names at heavily discounted prices – the best is Loehmann's in **Chelsea**. If you are the type who just loves searching for bargains, you will find this the most exciting shopping experience in town.

Electronics:

Electronic goods, from cameras to computers, are often considerably cheaper in New York but it pays to shop around. Shops on Fifth and Sixth Avenues advertising 'closing down sales' have been doing the same for years and the prices are not necessarily that cheap, nor the quality that good. Always compare the prices with those in a more mainstream store, and bargain if necessary. Remember too to make sure that the equipment is compatible with your system back home. There are several **discount electronics stores** on **Canal Street**, between Essex and Ludlow; a more reliable option might be Nobody Beats the Wiz (*726 Broadway at Waverley Pl*).

Fakes:

If you absolutely must have a fake Rolex watch or Mont Blanc pen, the place to go is Canal Street, between SoHo and Chinatown.

Eating out

It really doesn't make sense to talk about a New York style of cooking. In a single weekend, if you wanted, you could have dim sum *in Chinatown,* spanakopita *(spinach pie) in Astoria,* mondongo *(tripe soup) in Washington Heights and* zakuski *(Russian starters) on Brighton Beach. You could brunch on* tapas*, dine on the finest* sushi *and wind up in the middle of the night with a corned beef on rye.*

Many New Yorkers have simply forgotten how to cook. They eat out three times a week on average and the rest of the time they pick up a take-away. Even when they give a dinner party, they order the food from **Zabar's** or **Balducci's**. When the world's finest cuisines are available on your doorstep, there is little incentive to do anything else.

It is easy to be bewildered by the sheer range of choice. You want Afghan, Moroccan, Brazilian or Thai? Wholewheat or rye bread? Eggs over easy or sunny side up? How do you like your burger cooked, or your salad dressed? Do you want regular coffee, or half and half? Americans are used to making these choices; visitors have to learn them fast.

There are three basic types of cooking that crop up all over the city. One is the standard **American** fare of burgers, steaks and fries, found in cheap-and-cheerful diners in every neighbourhood. These retro establishments often have formica tables, chrome bars and surly waitresses who will top up your coffee over and over but will not hesitate to put you down if you ask for a double tall with foam. Secondly, there is **New American**, with French, Italian and Pacific Rim influences, an eclectic and highly personal style practised by most of the city's top chefs.

Finally, and most essentially New York, is the food brought over by **Jewish** immigrants at the end of the 19th century. Bagels, pastrami and lox have all become symbols of New York, but the words are Yiddish and their origins are in Europe. On top of all this are the regional American cuisines, from Cajun to Tex-Mex and the 'soul food' of the Deep South.

Choosing a **restaurant** can be a time-consuming business. Check the listings in the area chapters of this book. Look in *Time Out New York*, which lists its TONY 100 each week. If you are really serious about eating out, get hold of the food-lovers' 'bible', *Zagat's New York City Restaurants*, now in its 20th year. You can go to *www.zagat.com* This not only rates every restaurant by price and quality, but lists them by neighbourhood, style of cuisine and categories ranging from 'outdoor dining' to 'people-watching' and 'romantic spots'. Use it to find out which places are currently 'hot', but remember that this can change faster

than you can say Union Square Café. Be aware, too, that the hottest restaurants may require reservations weeks in advance – or may not take bookings at all. You can always just go for a cocktail at the bar, and still enjoy the views from the Rainbow Room or the River Café.

Fortunately, there is no need to go to expense-account establishments – just wander down any street and you will find something that takes your fancy. It is possible to eat well in New York on just about any budget. **Pushcarts** sell hot dogs, pretzels and slices of pizza; salad bars offer soup and salad, paid for by weight. **Chinese and Indian restaurants** are always a good bet for a reasonably priced lunch. In summer, pick up a picnic from one of the numerous delis, where the sandwiches are like skyscrapers; or splash out on chicken cacciatore and onion-crusted salmon from a high-class delicatessen like **Zabar's** or **Dean & Deluca**.

The lowdown

Although many restaurants are open all day and some stay open all night, the standard **hours** are around 1200–1400 for lunch and 1800–2200 for dinner. Many restaurants offer a **weekend brunch** which runs from around 1100–1600.

A growing number of restaurants offer a **prix fixe menu** at lunchtime and during the early evening 'pre-theatre' period. This can be a good way of trying some of New York's most celebrated restaurants at an affordable price.

Tipping generally varies between 15 to 20 per cent. The easiest way to work out your tip is to double the 8.25 per cent sales tax on your bill, then adjust up or down according to the quality of the service.

Since 1995, **smoking** has not been allowed in restaurants with over 35 seats. You may be allowed to smoke at the bar, but it is worth checking the arrangements when you book.

Drinking

The minimum drinking age is 21 and even if you are well over this age you may be asked to show your passport to prove it. **Beer** is mostly chilled American lager, though there has been a growing interest in microbrews and Brooklyn now has its own brewery. Some of the more traditional Manhattan pubs, like McSorley's Old Ale House and Pete's Tavern, also brew their own beers. **Wine** mostly comes from California or Washington State, though the top restaurants feature wines from France and around the world. Hotel bars and fashionable restaurants are the best places to drink **cocktails** such as Manhattan (whisky, lemon juice and vermouth) or Martini (always served with gin). From Monday to Friday some of the midtown hotels put out hot *hors d'oeuvres* during the after-work 'happy hour'; for the (high) price of a cocktail you can save the cost of an evening meal. It's probably a good idea to put on a jacket and tie.

Coffee is available everywhere, with free refills the norm. In recent years there has been an explosion of Starbucks coffee shops, offering lattes and other speciality coffees. For a decent cup of **tea**, your best bet is to splash out on afternoon tea at one of the swanky Upper East Side hotels (*page 117*).

A glossary of New York food terms

bagel	A chewy bread roll, boiled and then baked, often toasted and served with lox and cream cheese
bialy	A Jewish onion roll originating in Poland
blintz	Pancake filled with cheese or fruit and eaten with soured cream
collard greens	Boiled spiced cabbage from the American Deep South
egg cream	A deli drink consisting of iced milk soda with vanilla or chocolate
grits	Crushed maize porridge served with butter
gumbo	A thick Cajun soup, usually made with seafood and tomatoes
jerk	A spicy Caribbean marinade for chicken, beef or pork
knish	A Jewish pastry filled with cheese, buckwheat or potato
lox	Smoked salmon
pastrami	Smoked and seasoned beef
pierogi	A baked dough envelope stuffed with meat, cheese or potato
pretzel	A savoury twist of glazed pastry, usually sold from pushcarts
soda	Any soft drink (eg Cola, mineral water)

New York with children

Children love New York. They love climbing the skyscrapers and riding the Staten Island ferry. They love sitting on Hans Christian Andersen's knee in Central Park. They love the subways, the taxis and the hot dog carts, and the Statue of Liberty standing in the harbour. Seen through a child's eyes, New York is a magical place.

Many of the attractions in this book are suitable for children. Young children enjoy the fire engines at the **New York City Fire Museum** (*page 64*). Kids of all ages are fascinated by the dinosaurs at the **American Museum of Natural History** (*pages 132–133*) or the real-life animals at the **Central Park Wildlife Conservation Center** (*page 134*) and **Bronx Zoo** (*page 166*). Teenagers like shopping for CDs at the Virgin Megastore, or hanging out in the theme restaurants on 57th Street (*page 107*). Everyone loves **Coney Island** (*page 165*). The following activities are particularly suitable for children.

Big Apple Circus
All ages. Tel: 212–721–6500. If you're in New York at Christmas, try to catch this wonderful circus show, which runs from November to January at the Lincoln Center. Other seasonal events for kids are the **Nutcracker** (*ages ten and up*), also at the Lincoln Center, and the **Radio City Christmas Spectacular** (*ages three and up; tel: 212–247–4777*).

Brooklyn Children's Museum
*Tel: 718–735–4400. All ages. 145 Brooklyn Ave. Subway: 3 to Kingston Ave. Open: Wed–Fri 1400–1700, Sat–Sun 1000–1700. Admission: *.*
This was the first children's museum in the world when it opened in 1899. It is now housed in a futuristic building full of hands-on educational activities.

Children's Museum of Manhattan (*see page 136*).

FAO Schwarz
5th Ave at 58th St. Try not to bring your kids here until the end of the holiday. New York's most famous toy store has entertainers and storytellers, elevators that look like robots and gifts ranging from cuddlies to electronic toys.

Kid City
Ages three and up. At the New York Historical Society (page 137).

New Amsterdam Theater
214 W 42nd St. Tel: 212–307–4100. This landmark Art Deco theatre has been renovated by the Disney corporation and now features lavish Broadway productions suitable for families.

New Victory Theater
209 W 42nd St. Tel: 212–239–6200. The opening of this children's theatre in 1995 was a clear sign that Times Square was changing. Everything here is child-oriented and the tickets are a lot more affordable than for most Broadway shows.

New York Skyride
*Ages six and up. At the Empire State Building. Open: 1000–2200 daily. Admission: ***.* Crash on Wall Street and ride the Coney Island Cyclone on this seven-minute wide-screen simulation.

Prospect Park
Subway: D, Q to Prospect Park. Brooklyn's equivalent to Central Park offers fun and games for children of all ages. The **Prospect Park Wildlife Center** was reopened in 1995 as a

children's zoo; outside the gates is a vintage Carousel which is still in operation. **Lefferts Homestead** is a Dutch colonial farmhouse filled with hands-on children's activities, and storytelling beneath the tree on summer Sunday afternoons. The park itself is well supplied with 'tot lots' and grassy play areas, and the nearby **Botanic Garden** has a family nature trail and a discovery area where toddlers are encouraged to touch and smell the plants.

Sony IMAX Theater
Ages three and up. Broadway and 68th St. Tel: 212–336–5000. Children will gaze in wonder at this eight-storey screen, offering 3-D films of Manhattan as well as other features. Call ahead for show times and tickets.

Sony Wonder Technology Lab
Ages four and up (page 99).

Staten Island Children's Museum
*Tel: 718–273–2060. All ages. At Snug Harbor Cultural Center. Bus: S40 from Staten Island ferry terminal. Open: Tue–Sun 1200–1700. Admission: *.* This interactive museum, in a peaceful area of gardens and harbour views, makes a fun way to round off a trip on the Staten Island ferry.

After dark

Ask New Yorkers their idea of a perfect evening and it will probably involve curling up on the sofa with a good book. In a city saturated with culture, staying in has become the new going out. Sometimes it is possible to have just too much choice. With Hollywood actors playing Broadway and Pavarotti appearing at the Met, there may be as many as a dozen world-class performances in Manhattan on a single night. Faced with such a choice, the easiest thing is to stay at home.

But New Yorkers do go out, and so should you. From glittering first nights at the Met to gritty avant-garde theatre in East Village lofts, New York is the cultural capital of the world. Movies are shown here long before anywhere else; Off-Broadway theatres feature the big names of tomorrow. From hip-hop to modern dance, whatever trends are happening, you can be sure that they will be happening first in New York.

To find out what's on, check the listings in *Time Out* or pick up a free copy of *Village Voice* from clubs and bars in Greenwich Village. Another good source of information is the *New York Times*, especially the Friday *Weekend* section and Sunday's *Arts & Leisure*. Besides the major productions, look out for free or cheap events in churches, museums and parks. One thing you definitely should not miss is **Shakespeare in the Park**, which takes place in Central Park between June and September (*page 135*).

Cabaret

The days of Cole Porter and George Gershwin may be over, but cabaret is enjoying a revival in New York as a new generation of singers moves into the piano clubs and cocktail bars. Most are in swanky uptown joints like Café Carlyle, where you pay a hefty cover in the hope of seeing Woody Allen; alternative West Village cabaret venues like Bar d'O and Duplex feature camp comedians and drag queens singing Billie Holliday.

Arci's Place
450 Park Ave S (between 30th and 31st Sts). Tel: 212–532–4370.

Café Carlyle
Carlyle Hotel, E 76th St at Madison Ave. Tel: 212–744–1600.

Duplex 61
Christopher St. Tel: 212–255–5438.

Michael's Pub at the Park
Lombardy Hotel, 109 E 56th St. Tel: 212–758–2272.

The Oak Room
Algonquin Hotel, 59 W 44th St. Tel: 212–840–6800.

The Rainbow Room
30 Rockefeller Plaza, 65th Floor. Tel: 212–632–5000.

Don't Tell Mama
343 W 46th St (between 8th and 9th Aves). Tel: 212–757–0788.

Clubs

Manhattan's club scene changes faster than a set of traffic lights and the only way to find out what's hot is to ask around or pick up a copy of *Paper* magazine or the gay magazine *HX*. As a rule, fashion fascism is out and most clubs happily play host to a mixture of yuppies, homeboys, babes and drag queens. Gay is definitely in and the gayest clubs are also the most fun. Most clubs have theme nights on different days of the week, appealing to very different crowds, so it pays to check in advance. Theme nights at Mother, in the ultra-hip meatpacking district, include Friday's Clit Club for women and Saturday's cyber-fetish Click & Drag. Not much happens before midnight, even during the week. Expect to be frisked for drugs and bottles on the door, and bring along ID if you look anything like 21.

Vinyl
6 Hubert St at Hudson St. Tel: 212–343 1379.

Zanzibar
645 9th Ave at 45th St. Tel: 212–957–9197.

Tonic
107 Norfolk St (between Delancey and Rivington Sts). Tel: 212–226–8900.

Dance

The New York City Ballet begins its winter season each year with *The Nutcracker* and follows up with a spring season from April to June. The other leading company is the American Ballet Theater, which takes over the Metropolitan Opera House each spring with an emphasis on classical ballet. For experimental and modern dance productions, try the Dance Theater Workshop or the Brooklyn Academy of Music.

American Ballet Theater
Metropolitan Opera, Lincoln Center. Tel: 212–362–6000.

Brooklyn Academy of Music
30 Lafayette Ave. Tel: 718–636–4100.

City Center Theater
131 W 55th St. Tel: 212–581–1212.

Dance Theater of Harlem
466 W 152nd St. Tel: 212–690–2800.

Dance Theater Workshop
219 W 19th St. Tel: 212–924–0077.

Joyce Theater
175 8th Ave at 19th St. Tel: 212–242–0800.

New York City Ballet
New York State Theater, Lincoln Center. Tel: 212–870–5570.

Music – classical and opera

The Metropolitan Opera and New York Philharmonic perform at the Lincoln Center (*pages 136–137*), along with several other ballet, modern dance and opera companies. Both the Met and the Philharmonic also give free summer concerts in Central Park, which attract up to half a million spectators. Another major venue is Carnegie Hall (*page 90*), which has the best acoustics in the city. For something a little different, head across the water to Brooklyn for chamber music at Bargemusic beneath the Brooklyn Bridge, or seek out a cutting-edge performance at the Brooklyn Academy of Music – America's oldest opera house and the venue for the acclaimed Next Wave festival each autumn.

Bargemusic
Fulton Ferry Landing. Tel: 718–624–4061.

Brooklyn Academy of Music
30 Lafayette Ave. Tel: 718–636–4100.

Carnegie Hall
154 W 57th at 7th Ave. Tel: 212–247–7800.

Juilliard School of Music
Lincoln Center, Broadway at 65th St. Tel: 212–769–7406.

Metropolitan Opera
Lincoln Center. Tel: 212–362–6000.

New York City Opera
New York State Theater, Lincoln Center. Tel: 212–870–5570.

New York Philharmonic
Avery Fisher Hall, Lincoln Center. Tel: 212–875–5030.

Music – rock, pop and jazz

The jazz scene has drifted downtown since the days when Duke Ellington played the Cotton Club and the best clubs are now in Greenwich Village (*page 68*). One exception is the

Knitting Factory, which showcases experimental jazz even further downtown in trendy TriBeCa. In the Village, the big names play at the Blue Note and Village Vanguard but there are plenty of smaller clubs where you can hear jazz without paying a cover. Look out too for Jazz at the Lincoln Center, a summer festival directed by Wynton Marsalis. The biggest rock bands appear at Madison Square Garden, a huge 20,000-seater arena and sports stadium, but for something more cutting edge, check out CBGB in the East Village, the birthplace of American punk. For hip-hop, blues and a look at the stars of tomorrow, don't miss Amateur Night at the Apollo Theater in Harlem.

Apollo Theater
253 W 125th St. Tel: 212–222–0992.

Blue Note
131 W 3rd St at 6th Ave.
Tel: 212–475–8592.

Carnegie Hall
154 W 57th at 7th Ave.
Tel: 212–247–7800.

CBGB
315 Bowery at Bleecker St.
Tel: 212–982–4052.

Knitting Factory
74 Leonard St. Tel: 212–219–3055.

Madison Square Garden
7th Ave at 33rd St.
Tel: 212–465–6741.

SOBs
204 Varick St at Houston St.
Tel: 212–243–4940.

Sweet Basil
7th Ave at Bleecker St.
Tel: 212–242–1785.

Village Vanguard
7th Ave at 11th St.
Tel: 212–255–4037.

Theatre

Most Broadway productions take place every night of the week, with matinees on Wednesday, Saturday and Sunday (for an explanation of Broadway, Off-Broadway and Off-Off-Broadway, and details of how to get tickets, *see pages 108–109*).

Accommodation

New York has something for everyone looking for a place to stay. In addition to the top hotels, there are many hotels in the budget category that offer good value.

Paramount Hotel

Budget

YMCA Vanderbilt entrance

Pickwick Arms entrance

Washington Square Hotel entrance

Wellington entrance

Gershwin lounge

Beacon
2130 Broadway. Tel: 212–787–1100.
The smartest of the budget hotels on the West Side, the Beacon is named after the famous theater next door.

The Comfort Inn
42 W 35th St (5th and 6th Ave).
Tel: 800–567–7720.
Located in Midtown Manhattan near Macy's and the Empire State Building. Affordable New York charm coupled with European intimacy.

Edison
228 W 47th St. Tel: 212–840–5000.
This vintage building is one of the best value hotels in the theater district. The Art Deco lobby and brass doorways of the original 1931 hotel have all been beautifully restored.

Gershwin
7 E 27th St at Fifth Ave.
Tel: 212–545–8000.
www.gershwinhotel.com.
Located in the heart of the Flatiron district. The lobby shines with original pop art, including an actual Campbell's soup can autographed by Andy Warhol.

Grand Union
34 E 32nd St bet. Madison & Park
Ave. Tel: 212–683–5890. E-mail:
grandunionhotel@aol.com.
Located in Manhattan two blocks from the Empire State Building. The hotel offers a traditional style of elegance.

On the Avenue Hotel
2178 Broadway at 77th St.
Tel: 212–362–1100. E-mail:
ontheave@stayinny.com.
Located in Manhattan's Upper West Side. All rooms feature original ink and watercolor drawings by famed native artist Alfonso Munoz.

Pickwick Arms
230 E 51st St. Tel: 212–355–0300.
This is the best budget hotel in Midtown. There is a decent coffee-shop, a Spanish restaurant and an attractive rooftop garden.

Washington Square Hotel
103 Waverly Place.
Tel: 212–777–9515.
www.washingtonsquarehotel.com.
A highly recommended place, Washington Square Hotel, is in the heart of Greenwich Village. The cozy hotel has a European feel and style.

Wellington
871 7th Ave at 55th St.
Tel: 212–247–3900.
www.wellingtonhotel.com.
The Wellington, located on the West Side across from Carnegie Hall has beautifully decorated rooms and suites.

YMCA Vanderbilt
224 E 47th St.
Tel: 212–756–9600.
www.ymcanyc.org.
The best YMCA of NY City. Newly renovated rooms, includes disabled access.

Standard

The Franklin entrance   The Mansfield entrance hall   The Mansfield room   Paramount façade   Paramount room

Bedford
118 East 40th St. Tel: 212–697–4800.
www.bedfordhotel.com.
The Bedford is located two avenues from the New York Public Library and Fifth Avenue.

The Dylan
52 East 41st St. Tel: 212–338–0500.
www.dylanhotel.com.
The Dylan, located 9 miles from La Guardia Airport, offers everything for travellers who appreciate classic style.

The Empire
44 W 63rd St. Tel: 212–265–7400.
Recently renovated, this hotel has the look of a Tudor castle. It is close to the Lincoln Centre and the Empire Café is convenient for pre-dinner dining.

The Franklin
164 East 87th St. Tel. 212–369–1000.
www.franklinhotel.com.
The Franklin offers style, convenience and value on the Upper East Side, within a short walk of the Museum Mile, movie theatres and restaurants.

The Hudson
58th St. Tel: 212–554–6000.
www.hudsonhotel.com.
The Hudson Hotel's decor is captivating. Westside rooms offer a stunning view of the Hudson River.

Iroquois
49 W 44th St. Tel: 212–840–3080.
www.iroquoisny.com.
This hotel is well located for shoppers and theatre-goers. James Dean stayed here for a few years in the 1950's.

The Mansfield
12 W 44th St. Tel: 212–944–6050.
www.mansfieldhotel.com.
Conveniently located for theatre-goers. As a guest you will experience New York's world renowned 21 Club Restaurant.

Paramount
235 W 46th St. Tel: 212–764–5500.
This hotel is well designed and considered very trendy. The bar, known as Whiskey is one of the hot spots in town.

The Roger Williams
131 Madison Avenue (at 31st St).
Tel: 212–448–7000.
www.rogerwilliamshotel.com.
Designed by the renowned architect Rafael Viñoly, The hotel delivers a modern and harmonious environment.

The Shoreham Hotel
33 West 55th St. Tel. 212–247–6700.
www.shorehamhotel.com.
Located in the heart of midtown Manhattan, within a short walk of the finest Fifth Avenue shops, Central Park, Broadway Theaters and Carnegie Hall.

Hotel Wales
1295 Madison Ave.
Tel. 212–876– 6000.
www.waleshotel.com.
The Wales offers charm and nice views of Central Park.

Deluxe

Carlton façade   Michelangelo   Royalton room   Royalton bar   Royalton façade
                  entrance hall

Avalon
16 E 32nd St. Tel: 212–299–7000.
www.theavalonny.com.
The Avalon is situated just minutes
from Penn Station and the Empire
State Building. The layout and design
of the hotel blend traditional European
grandeur, boutique intimacy and top
of the line business amenities.

Carlton
22 E 29th St. Tel: 212–532–4100.
The Carlton is a stylish Beaux Arts
building and was recently renovated
and transformed into a first class hotel.
Conveniently located near 34th street.

Doral Tuscany
120 E 39th St. Tel: 212–686–1600.
The Doral Tuscany is an elegant Hotel
in Murray Hill. Guests can use the
Doral Fitness centre across the street.

Double Tree Guest Suites
1568 Broadway. Tel: 212–719–1600.
The Double Tree is beautifully located
in the Theater District. Guests will find
spacious quarters and a quiet haven
from the busy outside world.

Michelangelo
152 W 51st St. Tel: 212–765–1900.
A classy hotel situated off Broadway,
you can choose rooms according to
your taste in décor – Empire, Country,
French, or Art Deco.

Morgans
237 Madison Avenue at 37th St.
Tel: 212–686–0300.
The Morgans is a superior first-class
hotel located between Thirty-Seventh
and Thirty-Eighth on Madison Avenue
and it proudly features the Famous
Asia de Cuba restaurant.

The Plaza Hotel
768 Fifth Ave. (59th St).
Tel: 212–759–3000.
The Plaza was built with all the pomp,
glory, and opulence of a French chateau.
The Plaza's four restaurants are built to
cater to the different tastes and moods
of their clientele.

Royalton
44 W 44th St. Tel: 212–869–4400.
The Royalton has a space-age lobby,
curving hallways and rooms that look
like cabins on a sleek ocean liner.
The hotel attracts many celebrities.

60 Thompson
60 Thompson. Tel: 212–204–6464.
www.60thompson.com.
Located in Greenwich Village, this new
hotel offers its guests a quiet retreat
filled with sumptuous designs and
amenities.

Waldorf-Astoria
301 Park Ave. Tel: 212–355–3000.
www.waldorf.com.
This is truly a magnificent hotel and
restored to its 1931 Art deco glory.
The Peacock Alley is still very popular
to go for drinks.

Practical information

Practical information

Animals and pets

Pets are not usually allowed on buses and subways or in cabs unless they are for the use of assisting a disabled person. Taxi drivers may occasionally allow pets into their vehicles but it would not be safe to assume that all of them will.

Climate

New York's climate veers between extremes. In summer, the heat and humidity become stifling and oppressive, and anybody who can afford to, decamps to Long Island to take advantage of its cool Atlantic breezes. The air-conditioning in Manhattan is turned on so high that it can actually feel cold inside the shops. Winters are the opposite, laced with a bitter chill – and the buildings are heated to the point of exhaustion. The most pleasant times to visit are in spring (April to June), when cherry blossom blooms in the parks, and fall (September to November), when the crisp, sunny days bring out the colours of the autumn foliage. But New York is fun at any time of year. The summer holiday season, which begins with Memorial Day in late May and ends with Labor Day in September, is the time for picnics, boat rides and Shakespeare in Central Park; while winter, especially the period from Thanksgiving to Christmas, is for many visitors the most romantic time of all. The shops are full of tempting window displays, a giant snowflake hangs over 57th Street, *The Nutcracker* is on at the Lincoln Center and at the

Rockefeller Center you can ice-skate beneath a huge Christmas tree. Average maximum daily temperatures are 40°F (5°C) in February, 71°F (21°C) in May, 83°F (28°C) in August and 54°F (12°C) in November. Rain is likely at any time of year but particularly in early spring, and snow can fall between December and April.

Currency

The US dollar ($) is divided into 100 cents. Bills, which come in denominations from $1 to $100, are all the same size and colour so it is essential to take care and to examine your change carefully. Each coin has its own particular slang term – a cent is a 'penny', 5 cents is a 'nickel', 10 cents is a 'dime' and 25 cents a 'quarter'. A dollar is also known as a 'buck'.

Travellers' cheques in US dollars are widely accepted in lieu of cash in department stores, restaurants and hotels. Most transactions over about $20, though, are carried out by **credit card**. Your credit card can also be used (with a PIN number) to obtain cash from ATMs (automated teller machines), which operate 24 hours a day.

Customs regulations

Travellers arriving in the United States need to complete a customs declaration form, which is handed to a customs officer as you pass through immigration. You may bring in up to $100 of gifts

($400 for US citizens), plus 200 cigarettes (or 100 non-Cuban cigars) and one litre of alcohol. The importation of fresh food products and plants is strictly prohibited. When leaving New York, it is important to check the restrictions applying in your own country. As a rule, if you have made expensive purchases like jewellery or fur you will be expected to pay **import duty** on your return home.

spend a lot of time waiting at traffic lights between blocks.

Since 1993, all new buildings have been required to provide wheelchair access, and most older buildings have been adapted. A number of **Broadway theatres** also provide special services for hearing and visually impaired guests. A volunteer 'greeter' is available who understands the needs of disabled visitors and acts as an

Disabled travellers

Although facilities are improving all the time, getting around New York remains a serious challenge for disabled people. Few **subway stations** are fully wheelchair-accessible; those that are are marked on the subway map (*for up-to-date information, call 718–596–8585*). **Buses** are more practical – most have wheelchair lifts in the centre door – but are a very slow way of getting about. **Taxis** are required to pick up a passenger with a collapsible wheelchair, but many do not and few are equipped with wheelchair lifts. For short distances, the sidewalk is best, though you will

excellent source of information about the city for disabled people.

Electricity

The electrical current is 110–120V AC, and the plugs use two flat prongs. It is essential to use an adaptor plug and voltage converter if bringing higher-voltage items from other countries.

Entry formalities

Under the **Visa Waiver Program**, citizens of the UK, Ireland, Australia, New Zealand, Japan and most countries of the European Union do not need a visa for non-working visits to the United States of less than 90 days. You do need a full **passport**, valid for the entire 90-day period, and a return ticket to your home country. Canadian and Mexican citizens merely need to show an identity document, preferably a passport. Citizens of all other countries require a **visa**, available from your nearest US Embassy. You should allow up to a month for your visa application to be processed.

Health and insurance

Public and private health care in the United States can be extremely expensive, so it is vital to have a comprehensive **travel insurance** policy, providing at least $1 million of medical cover as well as cancellation, theft and personal liability insurance. In non-emergency situations it is always advisable to contact your insurers before arranging to see a doctor. In an **emergency**, you can call an ambulance by dialling 911.

Medicines are available at **pharmacies** and **drugstores**, though some which are sold over the counter in other countries may only be available on prescription in New York. If you are taking regular medication, try to bring an extra supply as well as a note or prescription from your doctor.

The rate of **HIV infection** in New York is extremely high and it goes without saying that you should take all the usual precautions. **Condoms** are available in pharmacies as well as in supermarkets and late-night delis and corner stores.

Information and media

New York's **tourist information office** is the **New York Convention and Visitors Bureau** (*810 7th Ave between 52nd and 53rd St; tel: 212–484–1200; open Mon–Fri 0900–1700*), where you can pick up maps, brochures and advice on all aspects of the city. The NYCVB also has a London office (*33 Carnaby St; tel: 0207–437–8300*). In New York, tourist information is also available from street kiosks (for instance, outside Grand Central Terminal, from the major department stores and from the new **Times Square Visitors Center** (*1560 Broadway between 46th and 47th St; open daily 0800–2000*).

For up-to-date information on events, nightlife and Broadway shows, you need to consult the local media. The *New York Times* is the paper of record, publishing 'all the news that's fit to print', as it proudly proclaims on its masthead, since 1851. With a mix of city, national and international news, this is the closest thing in America to a national **newspaper**. The Sunday edition, available on Saturday evenings, weighs in at 5 lbs and contains separate sections on everything from travel to real estate. The other daily papers are the

Daily News, a mid-market tabloid, and the *New York Post*, a sports-and-gossip tabloid owned by Rupert Murdoch.

Arts listings are published weekly in *Time Out New York*, an offshoot of its London namesake, and in the free paper *Village Voice*, available from clubs and bars and known for its left-leaning, pro-gay outlook. By contrast, the *New Yorker* is a venerable New York institution, with long intelligent features that are thoughtful and irreverent by turn. Between the two, *New York* magazine combines features on aspects of city life with entertainment, restaurant and nightlife listings. For the latest on the club scene, consult the monthly style magazine *Paper*.

Maps

The first thing to get hold of is a decent **subway map**, available from most subway stations as well as from information offices (*see above*). Deciphering the subway map is an art in itself but soon becomes an essential skill. The most important point to remember is that letters and numbers in bold indicate stops which are made at all times; light lettering indicates a part-time service. Forget this and you may find yourself on an express train whizzing past your destination.

A **bus map**, available from the same sources, is also useful for making connections, especially crosstown and in the far north of Manhattan. Street maps other than those in this book are

not really necessary as long as you remember the Manhattan grid system, which operates between 14th Street and Central Park, with Fifth Avenue as its central dividing line. An address given as 'W 42nd St' will be west of Fifth Avenue; 'E 42nd St' will be to the east. Most addresses are given as both an avenue and a street, enabling you to work out quickly and easily exactly where they are.

Opening times

Most **shops** are open from 1000 to 1800 Monday to Saturday, though many are also open in the evenings and on Sundays. Many midtown stores stay open until around 2000 on Thursdays. **Banks** are open from 0900 to 1500, Monday to Friday, though you can get money outside these hours by using your **credit** or **debit card** in a 24-hour **ATM** (automated teller machine). Museums are mostly closed on Mondays, but check the individual entries in this book. Many museums have one late-night opening day each week, when admission is generally reduced-price or free.

Public holidays

Banks, shops and businesses are closed on the following days. If any of these dates falls over a weekend then the holiday is held over until the following Monday.

1 Jan
New Year's Day

3rd Mon in Jan
Martin Luther King Day

3rd Mon in Feb
President's Day

Last Mon in May
Memorial Day

4 July
Independence Day

1st Mon in Sept
Labor Day

2nd Mon in Oct
Columbus Day

11 Nov
Veterans Day

4th Thur in Nov
Thanksgiving Day

25 Dec
Christmas Day

Reading

Novels

Henry James, *Washington Square* (1880): This comedy of manners reflects the moral dilemmas of upper-class New York life in the late 19th century. James himself grew up in a house on Washington Square.

Edith Wharton, *The Age of Innocence* (1920): This is considered the masterpiece of Wharton's novels about 'Old New York', which describe the high-society world of the 1870s. In 1993 it was made into a film by Martin Scorsese.

Betty Smith, *A Tree Grows in Brooklyn* (1943): This charming autobiographical novel about growing up in Brooklyn was turned into both a movie and a Broadway musical.

J D Salinger, *The Catcher in the Rye* (1951): The classic tale of adolescence follows teenager Holden Caulfield on his journeys of discovery through Manhattan. John Lennon's killer was carrying a copy of this book and told police that the motive for the murder could be found in its pages.

Jay McInerney, *Bright Lights, Big City* (1984): The leader of the 'Bratpack' group of novelists made his name with this book, which captures the fast-living, cocaine-snorting, yuppie lifestyle of the 1980s.

Travel writing

Jan Morris, *Manhattan '45* (1987): This semi-fictional account, based on later visits, attempts to recreate the optimism of New York during its Golden Age after the Second World War.

Nik Cohn, *The Heart of the World* (1992): The simple idea of a walk up Broadway allows Cohn to introduce an unlikely cast of real-life characters, from a Wall Street banker to a Dominican transvestite. This book teems with the manic energy of New York's streets.

Recent memoirs

Eddy L Harris, *Still Life in Harlem* (1996): This affectionate and honest memoir describes how Harlem has turned from the mecca of the black world into a symbol of urban despair –

and asks whether there is any hope for the future.

Daniel Drennan, *The New York Diaries* (1998): These 'too-true tales of urban trauma' began life as a website, describing the neuroses of late 20th-century New Yorkers living in a city where 'the housing situation forces people to read the obituary columns for real estate reasons'.

Marian Swerdlow, *Underground Woman* (1998): A fascinating account of four years on the subway by one of the first woman conductors in the early 1980s.

Films

Manhattan (1979): Woody Allen's eulogy to Manhattan, shot in black-and-white with a George Gershwin soundtrack, brilliantly captures the middle-class angst of the 1970s in a story of love, sex and analysis. If you see one film about New York, this should be the one.

Safety and security

New York is one of the safest cities in America (*see pages 140–141*), but it doesn't always feel that way – and there are still no-go areas that are best avoided after dark. The important thing is to keep your wits about you, know where you are at all times, and if a situation does not feel right then just walk away. Most New Yorkers have developed a sixth sense for danger and defence mechanisms to cope with it; you will notice, for example, that they rarely make eye contact with strangers on the subway. The more you look like a New Yorker, the less likely you are to be attacked.

In fact, if you keep to the main tourist areas of Manhattan and avoid poorly-lit

streets and parks at night, you are very unlikely to be **mugged**. Some people keep a wad of '**mugger's money**' in a separate pocket, just in case – but if a **mugger** discovers you have kept some money back, the consequences could be nasty. If you *are* attacked, the only sensible advice is to hand over *all* your money and then seek help from the police. You can help to reduce the danger by carrying as little cash as possible, not wearing ostentatious jewellery and looking as if you know where you are going even if you do not. If you are genuinely lost in what feels like a dodgy area, keep walking until you come to a subway station or to somewhere like a deli where you can ask for directions and help.

At **subway stations**, you will notice that many people stay in the 'Off Hour Waiting Area' by the ticket office until their train arrives rather than go down onto the platform alone. Once on the platform, head for the yellow sign marked 'During off hours train stops here'; this will ensure that you get on near the centre of the train, where the conductor's carriage is situated. If you still don't feel comfortable, especially late at night, take a cab.

quarter (25 cents) and keep a further stock of quarters handy in case your time runs out. For **long-distance** and **international** calls, the best option is a pre-paid **telephone card**, available from news kiosks and corner shops. These are issued by several different companies in denominations from $5 upwards and offer surprisingly good value – for example, a 30-minute call to Europe costs less than $5. Each card comes with its own individual PIN; you dial a freephone number, enter your PIN, then dial the number you want and a voice tells you how many minutes of credit you have. You can use phonecards from hotels to avoid the high surcharges imposed on international calls – though be aware that some hotels even make a charge for calls to toll-free numbers.

As in any large city, **pickpockets** are an ever-present danger. You can take obvious precautions such as not leaving a wallet in your back pocket, but remember to keep an eye on your possessions whenever you are in a crowded place and try not to get diverted by passers-by faking 'incidents' and then picking your pocket while your attention is elsewhere.

Telephones

There are public payphones on virtually every street corner in Manhattan, as well as in subway stations, restaurants and department stores. Although these are operated by a number of different companies, it makes little difference which one you use.

To make a **local call** within New York City, you need to deposit a

There are two main area codes in New York City, 212 for Manhattan and 718 for the outer boroughs. For calls within a single area – for example, calls within Manhattan – you should omit the area code and simply dial the last seven digits of the number. For calls from Manhattan to the outer boroughs and vice versa, first dial 1, then the area code and then the last seven digits. The same applies when calling other parts of the United States and Canada. Numbers beginning with 1-800 are toll-free. For **international** calls, dial 011, followed by the access code for the country you are calling (UK = 44), then the city or area code (minus the initial 0) and the local number.

You can contact the operator by dialling 0 and the **emergency services** on 911.

Time

New York is on Eastern Standard Time, five hours behind GMT and three hours ahead of Los Angeles. Daylight Saving Time, when the clocks are put forward one hour, operates between April and October.

Tipping

Just do it. Americans tip generously and many staff depend upon tips to supplement their wages – as they are often at pains to point out. You cannot expect to leave a bar without tipping and still get a smile from the bartender the next day. In **restaurants**, tip 15–20 per cent (a simple trick is to double the 8.25 per cent tax); in **bars**, a dollar a drink. **Taxi** drivers expect at least ten per cent, and **tour guides**, porters and **cloakroom attendants** should all get at least a dollar.

Toilets

The shortage of decent public toilets (known as 'restrooms' or 'bathrooms') in New York is so well known that there is even a book by the name of Where To Go. Virtually the only public restrooms are found in parks, and until recently these were more often than not a haunt for drug-dealers and unsavoury sexual predators. Things are gradually looking up, but your best bet for a toilet is still to saunter into the lobby of a midtown

hotel and look as if you know where you are going. Other good options are department stores; Barnes & Noble bookshops; museums; and the **New York Public Library**. Of course, you can always use the toilets in restaurants and bars, but be aware that these are often marked as being 'for patrons only' and you are expected to buy a drink.

Surf and go
useful websites

It is difficult to describe New York City – it is a world icon. With superb architecture, the world's greatest theatre district, some of the most renowned galleries and museums anywhere, eclectic neighbourhoods, diverse cultural events and fantastic restaurants – New York City has everything you could wish for. It would take a lifetime to experience it all, but for a good general introduction be sure to visit these websites to help plan your trip.

Accommodation

www.new.york.hotelguide.net
Listings of accommodation in New York are organised geographically and alphabetically.

www.bbonline.com/ny
A listing of bed and breakfast accommodation in New York City and its surroundings.

www.nyc.worldweb.com
This site has a good number of links to hotels and other types of accommodation in and around New York City.

www.yahoo.com
Go to the New York City link and click on lodgings. This is probably one of the best and most comprehensive listings of hotels, motels and bed and breakfasts in New York. You can even get a detailed description of the hotel.

www.expedia.com
Go to the New York City link for informative price comparisons on accommodation options.

www.aboutnewyorkhotels.com
A comprehensive listing of all types of hotels – from budget to luxury – in New York City.

www.travelzoo.com
Travelzoo lists the best prices, promotions and hot deals from hundreds of sites and consolidates them here.

www.nycresidence.com.
If you want to rent apartments and rooms instead of using a hotel, browse this site for good options.

TOP TIP

www.nycvisit.com
This is the website for the Official Visitor Information Centre (NYC & Company). It is the best website for a visit to New York, and it will save you time and trouble when choosing a place a stay. Getting to the link for hotels is a bit complicated, but once you're there you can view the hotel options by price, name or rating. Just type 'Hotels' in the search bar and follow the link that says 'Hotel Reservation Network'.

Travel and timetable information

www.panynj.gov
The official site of the Port Authority of New York and New Jersey, it provides information on shipping, terminals, bridges, tunnels, airports and waterfront development, and the Port Authority Bus Terminal. For information on any of the three airports, click on the 'Airport' link of this site. JFK Airport's official website is also linked to this site.

www.krusch.com/nysf.html
This is a New York City subway finder. This web server will give you subway directions to any Manhattan street in seconds.

www.si-web.com
Information about the Staten Island ferry.

www.amtrak.com
Amtrak online. Frequent trains to Washington DC and Boston depart from Penn Station.

www.jfk-new-york.com
Visit this site for information on car rentals and transportation from JFK Airport to your destination.

www.nycvisit.com
Use this site for any information about travel and transport.

TOP TIP

www.mta.nyc.ny.us
The official site of the Metropolitan Transport Authority, it is the most useful site for taking buses and subways in Manhattan, with easily-printable maps and updated information on any timetable changes. Do visit this site for updates on stations that are closing or re-opening – since 11 Sept 2001 there have been many changes in the subway system.

Sightseeing

www.citycenter.org

www.bigapplegreeter.org
Offers personal tours for small groups.

www.imar.com
Website of Insiders Marketplace – a group that offers hundreds of tours and other New York experiences.

www.newyorktalksandwalks.com
A multitude of seasonal, ethnic and historical tours.

www.circleline.com
Information on the tours (three-hour island cruises) that leave from Pier 83 at the west end of 42nd St, and Pier 16 at South St Seaport.

www.villagevoice.com
The *Village Voice* is the authoritative source on all that New York has to offer, and has a very good guide to entertainment.

www.timeoutny.com
The online version of 'The obsessive guide to obsessive entertainment'. This site is updated regularly for all-important listings of the city that never sleeps.

www.broadway.com
Visit this site for information on shows, reviews, venues and tickets. Also visit www.ticketmaster.com for deals.

www.zagat.com
Part of sightseeing is finding interesting places to eat. Come here for the best listing of food and restaurants in New York.

TOP TIP

www.nycvisit.com
Again, the best place to decide how, where and what to see in New York. Get great deals and discounts from this website.

Index

207

NEW YORK
Editorial, design and production credits

Project management: Cambridge Publishing Management Ltd.

Series editor: Gabriela Hallas

Copy editor: Rosalind Beckman

Proof-reader: Cambridge Publishing Management Ltd.

Series design: Trickett & Webb Limited and
Cambridge Publishing Management Ltd.

Cover design: WHSmith

Cover artwork: Cambridge Publishing Management Ltd.

Text layout: Cambridge Publishing Management Ltd.

Map work: RJS Associates and Cambridge Publishing Management Ltd.

Index: Richard Raper, Indexing Specialists

Repro and image setting: Cambridge Publishing Management Ltd.

Printed and bound by: Artes Gráficas Elkar, Loiu, Spain

We would like to thank **Ethel Davies** for the photographs used in this book, to whom the copyright in the photographs belong, with the exception of the following:

Getty images: pages 17, 202–205

NYC and Company: pages 16, 95

Zaid Hamid: pages 14, 24, 49, 52, 58, 63, 65, 70, 80, 110, 189, 190, 191

We would like to thank the following hotels for kindly providing photographs for pages 188–191: **Paramount Hotel, Washington Square Hotel, Wellington Hotel, Gershwin Hotel, Hotel Mansfield, Hotel Michelangelo.**